Why Am I Crying?

A helpful & honest look at depression

Martha Maughon

Why Am I Crying?
© 1983, 1989 by Martha Maughon. All rights reserved.

Discovery House Publishers is affiliated with
RBC Ministries, Grand Rapids, Michigan 49512

Discovery House books are distributed to the trade exclusively by
Barbour Publishing, Inc., Uhrichsville, Ohio 44683

Unless indicated otherwise, Scripture is taken from the
HOLY BIBLE, NEW INTERNATIONAL VERSION.
© 1973, 1978, 1984 International Bible Society.
Used by permission of Zondervan Bible Publishers.

Library of Congress Cataloging-in-Publication-Data

Maughon, Martha.
   Why am I crying? : a helpful and honest look at depression / by
Martha Maughon.—[2nd ed.]
   p.   cm.

   ISBN: 0-929239-17-2

   1. Maughon, Martha—Mental health. 2. Depression, Mental—
   Patients—United States—Biography. 3. Christian life—1960—
   United States—Biography. I. Title.
RC537.M384   1989
616.85'27'0092—dc20   89-19681
[B]   CIP

Printed in the United States of America

07 08 09 /CHG/ 15 14 13

Contents

Acknowledgments

It is impossible for me to acknowledge all who have contributed to my life, and thus to this book. I do, however, want to thank all who may see their helpful influence in these pages, and the many who assured me of their prayers for *Why Am I Crying?* Specifically, I would like to express appreciation to Janice Barfield, who believed in my message and encouraged me to share it, to Juanita Sawyer, who typed my manuscript and prayed as she typed, and to *Decision* Magazine's School of Christian Writing, without which I may never have written a word.

I would also like to thank my family for their love and support, and it is to them that this book is affectionately dedicated.

Grover

Doug, Janie, Manda

Lonnie, Becky, Matt, Erin

Publisher's Foreword

Martha Maughon knows about the dark, painful struggles with mental and emotional difficulties. She has been there. Fighting the battles of anxiety, guilt, and low sense of self-worth, she has experienced the healing touch of God, who used counselors, therapists, writers, and loved ones to bring wholeness and health. All of this Martha shares in *Why Am I Crying*, the story of her pain and His grace.

We pray that the much-needed message of this book will encourage and enlighten those who face similar difficulties. Not all will be helped in the same ways, nor by the same sources, as was the author, but we trust God will use her narrative to give hope to those reading these pages.

—The Publisher

Foreword

This is a book that needed to be written. Martha Maughon has dealt with the very difficult area of mental and emotional illness without falling into simplistic explanations and pat answers. This book could not have been written by a professional but had to come from someone who has experienced deep depression. Because of her own suffering, the author is able to write as one who knows the true feeling and anguish of anxiety and depression, and she writes with much personal honesty, giving the book credibility and integrity.

Martha clearly demonstrates confidence in the love of God and the truth that if we submit to the leadership of Jesus Christ, He will bring something good out of our suffering. She shows that there is much hope for those who are depressed—hope from God and hope from loved ones, friends, and professionals who use their various gifts to support and minister to the depressed.

Why Am I Crying? offers real encouragement for those who suffer mentally and emotionally. It contains a message that needed to be delivered, and it is my pleasure to recommend it.

—James D. Mallory, Jr. M.D.

Introduction

When my mother was a little girl, she loved the name Martha. In fact she was so enchanted with this name that she gave it to her dolls as well as to her pets. Dogs, cats, and, I suppose, the mules, pigs, and all the other farm animals were named Martha. So it was not surprising that when her doctor announced, "It's a girl," she gave me the name she had tenaciously treasured for so long—the beloved name Martha.

When I was growing up, I didn't think very much about my name. Oh, I went through the typical girlhood stage of wishing I had been named Tonya or Deborah or something dramatic, but Martha was okay; I was used to the name, and it was mine.

As an adult, however, I find my name has taken on new significance because I have come to know another Martha—Martha of the New Testament. The more clearly I see this lady of Bethany, the more closely I identify with her. The Scripture portrays her as jittery, frustrated, obsessive, and, at times, complaining. She appears zealous, busy, striving for perfection.

Martha was concerned about what people thought. Had she lived with the pressures of today's society, she might have been set up for some psychological difficulty. She seemed to run the gamut of emotions, and I painfully recognize a reflection of myself as I see her bustle and struggle.

But Martha had something very powerful going for her. She had a special friend, Jesus, and He made the difference in her life. Jesus is my friend too, and His exhortation to Martha rings through time and infinity, and sinks deep into my soul as

I hear Him plead, "Martha, Martha, you are anxious and troubled about many things" (Luke 10:41 RSV). I, too, have had an anxious heart and a troubled spirit for most of my adult years.

In friendship Jesus has walked with me. In the dark and difficult times He has upheld me with His victorious right hand, and when I've grown weary, He has "let me rest in the meadow grass" (Ps. 23:2 LB).

In these pages I share my experience with anxiety and depression as openly and honestly as I can. No two of us walk exactly the same road. Each of us is unique—we come from different backgrounds and we have different experiences. It follows that our emotional experiences are different— even our depressions are different. I write about the difficulties that I encountered and the things that helped me. I have not intended to advance an academic dissertation on the principles of psychology or a scientific analysis of the cause and effect of human behavior. I am not qualified to handle any of that. There are many approaches to diagnosis and treatment of depression; many theories regarding cause and cure. I do not address these because my view would be unauthoritative and unbeneficial. This is simply my story—it is what happened to me. I tell it for no reason other than to encourage those who may be dealing with depression. And if only one person reading takes heart again, it will have been worth the telling.

May our friend Jesus hold you, dear reader, in the sunshine of His health and peace.

Martha, Martha

I can't help being a Martha sometimes, Lord.
When there's so much to do,
I worry and hurry
    to get the jobs done.
Yet the gentle call to sit at your feet
    is always in my mind.

Help me to trust you enough
    to turn loose the broom and the spoon
    and rest in your presence
        for a while each day,
Lest when I see you face to face,
I learn my striving counted for nothing.

—Martha Maughon

1

ANXIETY

The Dark Tormentor

Waking from a deep sleep, I could hear my own convulsive sobs, but it seemed as if they were coming from someone else. "Why am I crying? Where am I? What's wrong with me?"

As I pushed my way through the gloom and into consciousness, I could hear people around me talking. They were as puzzled by my uncontrolled crying as I was. "What's the matter with her? Is something wrong with her baby?"

"Oh, she's disappointed that the baby is a girl," an attendant answered back.

About that time a familiar voice spoke to me. My doctor was sternly instructing me to get control of myself. I realized that I was indeed the only one who could control my sobbing. Applying the old bootstrap principle, I strained to reach down into myself and pull. When I was able to stop the audible weeping, I began to recall the events that had led to that moment.

The evening before had been a typical mid-August night in Georgia—warm and still. Although I was rather great with child and two days past my due date, eleven o'clock found me puttering around the kitchen making cupcakes and cleaning up. The diet pills the doctor had prescribed had provided an abundance of extra energy, and I was planning what I would do when I finished in the kitchen.

Quite suddenly, labor contractions began at five-minute intervals. After only a few contractions, they jumped to three minutes apart and came regularly. I needed to get to the hospital posthaste. By the time my husband, Grover, grabbed my suitcase and we headed for the car, I could hardly walk. The pain was paralyzing, yet we did not realize how close to delivery I was. I had been in labor only about half an hour.

We were just a couple of miles from our house when it became obvious that our new little daughter was to become one whom Dr. Dobson would later refer to as a "strong-willed child," for she had no intention of waiting for the hospital. She would first see the light of day in the front seat of our Pontiac. The pains assailed, one immediately following the other. I felt as if my spine were being ripped from my body. I thought I was dying. We were frantic.

Many times I have cried to the Lord for help, but the volume and vigor I used on that night surpasses all other occasions, before or since. Grover, usually the conservative, defensive driver, leaned on the horn and ran all stop signs and red lights as we shot wildly up the road toward Atlanta.

We couldn't believe what was happening when the baby's head delivered, and she cried out. Grover whipped into the first place he saw with a telephone in order to summon help. It was a Texaco filling station—the only thing open at that time of night. Since I was not entirely familiar with the childbirth procedure, I feared the baby might be injured if too much time elapsed between the delivery of her head and complete delivery. So with all the strength and determination I could muster, I gave one great push. With a soft thud, precious little Becky hit the car seat.

It is important to remember that we were not one of the couples of the present generation who planned for the beautiful Lamaze natural childbirth procedure with breathing exercises, dim lights, and pleasant music. I'm talking about 1953 when we all enjoyed twilight sleep to have our babies. My sentiments paralleled those of Prissy in *Gone With the Wind:* "Lawsy, Miss Scarlet, I don't know nothing 'bout birthing babies."

Grover rushed back to the car to assure me that help was on the way. I boasted weakly, "Here's your baby." She was sleepy-eyed, contented, and apparently quite satisfied with the developments of the evening. Who needs a hospital anyway?

When the ambulance arrived, the attendant, a kind medical student, looked after our immediate needs. He helped me deliver the placenta and determined that it was complete. He recommended that we go on to the hospital for further examination and care. Placing a pill under my tongue, he wished us well and sent us on our way. Becky rested on my lap as we drove into the city. I felt only total exhaustion.

I guess I must have thought I had done something pretty special, delivering my own baby. The ambulance attendant had radioed the hospital that we were coming, and I expected cheers when we reached the hospital—or at least congratulations for a job well done. But our arrival went unnoticed, and I felt a little slighted. Grover's expedition to the emergency room resulted in an elderly man shuffling out with a stretcher. I dragged myself from the car and climbed onto the stretcher with my last bit of strength. Grover carried tiny Becky, who was loosely wrapped in a square piece of something from the ambulance. I flattened out on the stretcher and the little man pushed. We were quite a parade.

In the hospital I was sedated, examined, and repaired. It was the next morning that I woke up crying uncontrollably. The shock of the night before had left me traumatized. Unexplained panic so gripped me that I could only conclude that I was losing my mind. Since the feeling defied all description, I thought nobody would understand, so I decided to keep it to myself.

The day seemed ten years long. Lying in my semi-private room, I kept thinking about the night before. I didn't want to see the baby again, and that made me feel guilty. As the hours wore on, I learned that the hospital was not going to let me have Becky in my room. Since she was born outside the hospital, she could not come on the sterile floor where I was. She had been placed in a special nursery, and I could not go to her. Of course, when this was outlined to me, along with a few dozen assurances that "your baby is all right," I became desperate to see her. Was she really all right? Were they telling me the truth? I ached to hold her, to check her out. My anxiety increased.

Periodically all the little baby bassinets were rolled down the hall, and each baby was given to his or her mother. It would break my heart when my baby would not be with them. My roommate let me cuddle her little girl for part of the visiting time. It was a pitiful arrangement, but it helped.

Slowly the dreaded night nudged in. Family and friends who had helped me pass the day went home. The hospital fell into stillness, and only my fears and shattered nerves were left to keep me company. I seriously considered running up and down the halls screaming to see if it would alert someone to the fact that I had a deep and indescribable problem. But, of course, I was far too inhibited to do anything like that. Once I called the nurse and tried to tell her that I knew I was okay physically, but something was wrong with my mind. I asked her to find out if my doctor was still in the building, for I knew he sometimes stayed late for deliveries. She never came back.

I prayed that God would just help me go to sleep, for I had to stop thinking and feeling. Finally sleep came.

Day number two in Becky's life brought some relief. Dr. James Maughon, my brother-in-law, knew the doctor in the pediatric department at the hospital, and he got permission for Grover to wheel me to the hall where I could look at Becky through the window. It comforted me to see her sleeping there—all rosy and fat, with one foot propped on the side of the incubator, dreaming about the angels. She was the only well baby in that special nursery, and she looked wonderful! I knew then that she was all right, and somehow I would make it, too.

I know that a lot of women have delivered their own children without benefit of a hospital. Many of them have given birth under far worse circumstances than I did, and they have fared okay. My experience was not so unusual, but it was traumatic for me. The shock of self-delivery, the presence of the diet pills in my system, the feeling of failure in not presenting my husband with a son, the worried expressions on the faces of loved ones, the embarrassment of having given birth in the street, along with a number of negative incidents that occurred during my stay in the hospital were too much for my sensitive psyche. And it set off a full-blown neurosis.

There was no way I could have known the intense suffering that lay ahead for me. I left the hospital hoping that once I got home, the familiar routines and responsibilities would help me overcome my mental conflicts. I did settle in to a degree, but I maintained an underlying anxiety that I could not explain. Friends and family had no idea that I was struggling, and they constantly made jokes and teased me. Actually, much of what was said and done is funny to me now, and I recall some of the incidents quite vividly.

"Boy, have I heard a funny tale about you." The voice came from behind me in the grocery store; it belonged to the mother of a high-school pal.

"Oh really." I feigned a sick smile and hurried on my way hoping she wouldn't bother to tell me what she'd heard.

The word about Becky's birth was out, and I was the subject of all kinds of jokes and funny remarks. I received lots of notes and cards ranging from expressions of sympathy to "sorry about your accident." One day I got a picture of the Texaco advertisement that was popular at the time. It featured a cute little baby with a big Texaco Fire Chief hat sitting sideways on his head.

Tom, our friend across the street, excitedly approached Grover to hear the details. "I just can't believe this. I don't know what I'd do if it happened to me." He went on, "It really makes me nervous when I think of the possibility . . . " His voice trailed off.

"Well, Tom," my wise husband advised, "babies are born every day. You could see your wife through it if you had to."

"Oh, no," Tom exclaimed, "I don't mean that. I used to want to own a filling station."

Later when Grover was talking to another friend about Becky's birth, I heard him say, "I used to wonder how I would tie the cord if I ever had to help deliver a child, and I had decided I would use my shoestring. That night I looked down, and lo and behold, I was wearing loafers."

I laughed along with everyone else, but inside I felt embarrassed and ashamed.

The Dark Tormentor

Trying to get on with my routine life was a difficult problem. Janie, our older daughter, hit the "terrible two's" and wasn't the least bit excited about sharing her home with a little intruder.

As Becky matured she developed an obtrusive cavernous hemangioma (strawberry mark) right between her eyes, and we were having a terrible time getting it arrested.

Grover was working almost every night, and our church was encountering some serious problems. All of this added to my already pounding neurosis.

Day and night I was followed by a feeling of doom, and often, without provocation it seemed, I would be blasted with violent panic. I would flash back to the mental crash I had suffered in the hospital. In the panic I always feared that my mind was going—it was as if I could reach out and grab for it. The attacks were followed by depression and continued anxiety because I couldn't understand what was happening.

My only way of coping was to try to stay busy and involved with varied activities and wait for the extreme attacks to pass. I worked hard at putting aside the worst of the feelings, telling myself that someday it would get better. In retrospect, I don't know how I managed as long as I did with such overwhelming suffering.

As the days stretched into weeks I began to crumble with the strain. I couldn't eat; I couldn't sleep. Even breathing was difficult because my chest felt crushed by the torment of the fear. To describe it I wrote:

> *Who knows the dark tormentor?*
> > *That one who wrecks the plans of man*
> > *And slays the joys of life.*
> > *Who stalks his prey throughout the day*
> > *And hovers in the night.*
> *He sits heavy on my chest*
> > *Relentless,*
> > > *Robbing,*
> > > > *Mocking me.*
> *His name is Fear*
> > *And I know him well.*

Born out of my pessimism, it was a poem whose conclusion I would not be able to write until later.

Because I was a Christian, I looked to the Lord for healing and guidance, but the more I thought about Him, the more guilty and anxious I became. How could this be happening to me if I really belonged to God?

With regularity I reviewed some specifics in my spiritual pilgrimage. I attended a revival in my home church when I was nine years of age. At the time of the invitation I was impressed to "go forward" in response to the call to commit my life to

Jesus Christ. I understood very little about commitment, but as I grew older, I did understand—and I knew that I was holding out on God.

When I was nineteen and a bride of seven months, I took another step. I stood in the balcony of the great auditorium of the Baptist Assembly in Ridgecrest, North Carolina, listening to the hundreds of singing voices from the floor below.

I know not why God's wondrous grace
To me He hath made known,
Nor why, unworthy, Christ in love
Redeemed me for His own.

I know not how this saving faith
To me He did impart,
Nor how believing in His Word
Wrought peace within my heart.

I know not how the Spirit moves,
Convincing men of sin,
Revealing Jesus through the Word,
Creating faith in Him.

I know not when my Lord may come,
At night or noonday fair,
Nor if I'll walk the vale with Him,
Or meet Him in the air.

Then the beauty and significance of the refrain wafted its way into the balcony, into my heart, and, I am sure, into heaven itself:

But "I know whom I have believed,
and am persuaded that He is able
To keep that which I've committed
Unto Him against that day."

—Daniel W. Whittle

I knew I had to settle things with God. With unfeigning honesty I surrendered. "Father, I take my hands off my life. From this time forward in every way I know how, I give myself to You. I want to be who You want me to be, and I want to do what You want me to do."

It was like a step out into the sunshine, and my life was never the same again. I could say with the apostle Paul, "Old things are passed away; behold, all things are become new" (2 Cor. 5:17 KJV). I was at peace.

As I reflected on those experiences I could establish in my mind that though I had stumbled and fallen, I had never left that commitment. Why then, why had I lost the assurance, the joy of my salvation? Why did I feel so estranged from God, so frightened of His judgment, so futile?

I could only conclude that I must not be saved. Then, the harder I struggled to assure myself of my salvation, the more horrendous my illness became. Suicide seemed like a good option, except I was afraid to meet the Lord that way. I lived with these fears for two long years. As my condition grew steadily worse, I wished I had never been born.

Then one June afternoon—I remember it very well—I was sitting at my dresser, staring but not seeing. By then, I was obsessed with my condition. So I did what I had said I would never do. I gave up. It was as if something inside me clicked, and I slid into a deeper level of depression. After that it seemed that I was always miles away from everybody, everything was remote, and I was only a zombie. I never lost contact with reality—I believe to have done so would have been a relief. Indeed it was the reality that caused the pain.

Something Must Be Done for Martha

It was 1955. Becky was nearly two years old. I had come to the end of all trying. I had to find someone who would understand my desperation, someone who would help me.

A visit to my doctor resulted in a bottle of nerve pills and a jovial, "Honey, if you can't breathe, you aren't going to live very long." (No wonder I felt hopeless.)

My closest friends and loved ones knew I was having a hard time, and they tried to help in ways they understood. Grover was sympathetic. He helped with the girls and housework, listened to my groanings, took me out on the town. But he was just too close to the situation, and my decline had been so gradual.

I couldn't bring myself to go to my parents because I knew they would be hurt, and I couldn't bear seeing them disturbed by my problems. I knew that the only people who could understand my emotional suffering were those who had experienced it themselves or those who had made mental illness a field of study. At that time there was not as much known about mental illness as there is today, and it seemed that fewer people were plagued with it. I did not know one single person who had been through what I was going through.

But there was one person to whom I could go, someone who would help me. Grover's mother was a wise, strong, perceptive lady. She had reared five children and was the bulwark of the family. Mama was tough. I'd heard her tell about all the times the children had come in sick or with broken limbs or with heads split open and bleeding, and she would "just help put them back together and never get rattled."

Well, I sure had a "bleeding head," and *putting* back together was exactly what I needed. I steered a lifeless self over to my mother-in-law's house and found her sitting in the white swing in her lovely flower-lined backyard. "Mama," I cried, dropping down in the swing beside her. With uncontrollable sobs, I poured out my story, "There's something terribly wrong with me. I am going insane, and I can't do anything about it. Please get help. Please send me off somewhere."

It was obvious to Mama that I was sick and had reached a point far beyond that which laypeople are equipped to handle.

Immediately she found Grover and persuaded him, "Something must be done for Martha. She needs professional help, and there is nothing to be gained by waiting."

Years later I was counseling with a young woman who was suffering with extreme depression. When I asked her how her family was responding to her condition, she told me that she couldn't tell her mother-in-law what was wrong with her. "Oh, I could never tell her that," she said. "She would never understand, and she would be so embarrassed and upset!" I couldn't help but breathe a prayer of thanksgiving for the special mama-in-law God had given me.

With loving support, my family found a doctor, provided for my children, and took me to another city for treatment.

As Grover and I approached University Hospital, I stared at the great, red building with its picturesque twin-entrance front. It was stately and impressive as it loomed against the blue summer sky. But in my heart I doubted there was help in there for me. I was convinced that nobody had ever been in never-never land, where I was, and found their way back.

"Do you really want to get well?" the doctor asked as I sat before him crying again.

I choked out an earnest, "More than anything else in the world."

He spoke some soft words of encouragement, assuring me that they were going to help. He then told us that I would have to remain at the hospital for a while. This did not come as a surprise—we were prepared for it.

After our interview the doctor confided in Grover that I had only about a fifty percent chance of recovery. "It's her preoccupation with religion that concerns me," he stated. He said that he would prescribe electroshock therapy because mine was a deep and longstanding difficulty. He went on to explain, "Many times everything else will be removed from the mind, but religion will still be there." I have thought about his statement and wondered if perhaps it is evidence of the great power of all spiritual phenomena.

There I was. In a strange hospital, miles from home. I was sick and had been given a fifty percent chance of recovery and instructions that I could have no visitors. I was imprisoned behind locked doors, barred windows—and Grover left me there.

Perhaps He Wept Again

In the eleventh chapter of John we find these beautiful words, "Now Jesus loved Martha." Out of a holy, love-filled heart the Lord Jesus wept with Martha as she grieved for her dead brother, Lazarus. And that omnipotent love was strong and caring enough to deliver Lazarus from the bonds of death and present him well and whole to Martha and Mary, who cared for him so deeply.

I know the Lord's love had not diminished one bit as He looked down and saw me in my anguish, beaten to death emotionally and spiritually. Perhaps He wept again as He loved me with the same tenderness He had shown His friends at the sepulcher that day so long ago.

He kept watch over me when I could not be responsible for myself. By the time I reached the hospital, I was too ill to actively claim the power of that love, but that does not limit Jesus. And He was not concerned about the poor odds. In fact, I believe He likes them, for it is then He is able to show His greatest strength and power.

Those weeks spent in the psychiatric ward of a good hospital were part of God's answer to my prayers. My electroshock treatments began immediately and were given each day. This form of treatment is administered by sending convulsive doses of electricity through electrodes that are strapped to the patient's head. I was sedated and belted down before each treatment to avoid bone fracture at the time of convulsion. When the electricity passed through my brain, it

26

stabilized the neurotransmitter system and effected a temporary memory loss. This caused me to forget my harmful, obsessive thoughts and gave my mind an opportunity to rest. My doctor compared it to the removal of furniture from a room. "She will put it all back," he said. "But she'll put it back in a better place."

Shock therapy of all forms has fallen under a great deal of criticism in recent years and has largely been replaced by anti-depressant drugs and tranquilizers. Many therapists do not use shock at all, and some patients have come to fear it mainly because of its resultant progressive amnesia. Of course it is not a cure-all, but according to countless reputable psychiatrists it is effective in treating some types of depression. I didn't think it was so bad, and I would submit to it again should I ever find myself in a depressive state that is resistant to other forms of therapy.

"What is your name? Do you know who I am? Do you know where you are?" I heard these orientation questions daily as the doctors checked on my progress. At first I had difficulty with the answers, but eventually I could spout them off as quickly as the questions were asked, although I couldn't hold the thoughts in my mind for very long.

One day I awakened to find the doctor at my bedside. Lightly he asked, "How's your religion problem?"

I kidded, "Oh, did I tell you about that mess?"

He was delighted. The shocks had been effective. My disturbance, including my confusion about religion, had been temporarily interrupted, and I would have opportunity for a fresh perspective.

I recall only scanty details of the hospital experience. I remember kind personnel, good meals, table games for patient recreation, and becoming Chinese checker champion of the ward. I remember the way the room looked where we took the shock treatments, and the way the other patients looked when they were wheeled out of that room—flushed and still as death. But mostly I remember that I couldn't remember.

When the treatments were completed, I was dismissed from the hospital without further therapy. They seemed to think that I was a bright woman with a healthy lifestyle and would be able to work things out okay. That proved to be something of a fallacy, however, for although I was never that sick again, all of the difficulties that had set me up for that kind of a breakdown still had to be sorted out and dealt with.

The day I left the hospital everyone on the floor rejoiced with me. I was confused at that point and didn't understand why they sang out, "Goodbye, don't ever come back."

At home I tried to resume a normal life. The first few days I was happy— giddy is more like it. When talking, I often repeated myself, was forgetful, and giggled a lot. As a result of the treatments, I couldn't even recognize my own clothes in the closet, but that wasn't too bad—I'd never had a complete new wardrobe before!

Grover was gentle and kind. He would take me for a ride, take me to see friends, or take me anywhere I wanted to go. When he stood beside me, he appeared as proud as he did the day we married. I'll always love him for that, and only the passing of years has revealed just how important his affirmation and positive reinforcement were at that critical time of my life.

Other affirming experiences boosted my comeback from the pit. Once our pastor and his wife left their baby with me. I can still see that mother placing her son in a little car-bed just under the window in my living room and leaving him in my care. Of course they weren't gone very long, and they knew I was capable of looking after the baby, but a lot of people would not have trusted me then. I'm grateful for the confidence that Martha (for that was her name, too) placed in me that day and in the days that followed as she became a close and loving friend.

Gordon W. Allport said, "Love has been called the greatest therapeutic force of all."

That was certainly my experience. The loving gestures of my family, neighbors, and friends helped me as I slowly walked the road to recovery.

John Powell expands on this in *Why Am I Afraid to Love?* "We know that if the bud of a flower is injured by hostile forces, like an unseasonal frost, it will not open. So, too, a human person who is without the warm encouragement of love, and who must endure the chilling absence of praise and affection, will remain closed in on himself. The dynamics of his personality will be jammed. And, if the dynamics of his personality are seriously impeded, the result will be what psychologists call neurosis."

Even as love is imperative for any personality, it is of utmost urgency for persons with mental or emotional illness who often feel so unlovable. Since God knew that all the time, He commanded us to love one another. Paul tells us in 1 Corinthians 13 that love is kind. He also says, "In love you must serve one another, 'You must love your neighbor as yourself.' But if you snap at one another, and devour one another, you must watch that you do not end up by wiping out each other" (Gal. 5:13–15, *The Daily Bible Study Guide*, William Barclay).

The kindness expressed in love is stabilizing and curative, and its absence can be devastating. John Powell says, "We are, each one of us, the product of those who have loved us—or refused to love us."

A Cloud of Fear

Even though the shock treatments cleared up the very extreme aspect of my depression, as the temporary confusion and memory loss wore off, I became increasingly aware of the old, inordinate anxiety and depression that still had to be dealt with.

A picture of me in the ensuing years would have resembled the character in Li'l Abner who always had a cloud over his head. Although I was functioning in day-to-day activities, I never had a sense of well-being and was constantly followed by a cloud of fear and melancholy.

Although Dr. Gary Collins' book, *Christian Counseling*, was not available to me then, when I read it later I found this very accurate description of my feelings at that time. "Anxiety, stress, fear, tension—technically these words have different meanings, but they are often used interchangeably to describe one of the most prevailing characteristics of twentieth-century human beings. Psychologist Rollo May has called anxiety 'one of the most urgent problems of our day.' It has been termed the 'official emotion of our age . . . and the most pervasive psychological phenomenon of our time.' Although anxiety is as old as human existence, the complexities and pace of modern life have altered us to its presence and perhaps have increased its influence.

"Anxiety might be defined as an inner feeling of apprehension, uneasiness, concern, worry, and/or dread which is accompanied by heightened physical arousal. It can arise in reaction to some specific identifiable danger (many writers call this "fear" rather than anxiety), or it can come in response to an imaginary or unknown danger. This latter kind of anxiety has been termed 'free-floating.' The person senses that something terrible is going to happen but he or she does not know what it is or why."

Dr. Collins also says, "We might conclude that anxiety arises as a result of threat, conflict, fear, unmet needs, and individual differences." It seemed that I had all the kinds and all the causes of anxiety. Certainly it was chronic, it did float, and I had acute attacks. I recall days in which I would be afraid to move from one room to another. The advice to live "one day at a time" often became "fifteen minutes at a time." And I had absolutely no idea what the causes of my anxiety were.

The Quest

Once when I was chatting with Jim Maughon, he made the off-hand remark that "insight is the cure" for a troubled mind. This man is a physician and obviously he did not mean that insight is the total cure for all stress-related problems, but what he said triggered something in my mind. I was impressed—even excited—about the concept that this remark suggested. If insight is important to good emotional health, I could have some control over my future. Maybe I wouldn't have to feel bad for the rest of my life, because insights could be learned. From that moment I determined to find the answers for *me*.

Carl Jung in *Man in Search of a Soul* stressed the importance of gaining insight. He embellished the Scripture a bit and said that the most meaningful moments of his life were the moments of faith, hope, love, and insight.

I wanted to know how my past experiences had influenced me, how my present circumstances were afflicting me; I wanted to probe my feelings about the future. I became eager to explore my theological beliefs and misgivings. I began to read a great deal and talk with other people—all in an attempt to gain insight.

So my life became a quest. I searched for the realities that would promote healthy thinking and healthy behavior. I opened up to new insights. Frankly, in those early days my quest was for the things that would make me feel better. I was tired of a life of incessant gloom and conflict. I carefully watched for truths that I thought might be from God, for I believed then and I believe now, that if I lean heavily on Him, though I may not *feel* secure, He will not fail me.

I knew that if God is who He says He is, then His Word has to be true. And His Word promises me peace, assurance, wisdom, and a world of other blessings that I was obviously missing out on.

His Word also says, "You will know the truth, and the truth will set you free" (John 8:32). I wanted to know the truth, and I wanted to be free. As Jacob of old, I would wrestle with God until He blessed me.

Throughout the days of my quest God used a wide variety of methods to transmit His precepts and give me courage when the path was murky and bleak. On many occasions He used friends who shared openly their problems and insights they had learned. Christians who were willing to be transparent and honest about some of their own negative feelings were especially helpful.

It is a sad fact that we Christians sometimes retard healing in the lives of others because we refuse to be vulnerable. Someone has defined vulnerability as the "willingness to be wounded." So many times we are too proud or too frightened to let ourselves be known. We put on a victorious disguise and become so preoccupied with protecting our reputations as Christians we fail to be real. Since nobody can relate to an apparently problem-free person, we forfeit our opportunities to minister to the hurting others whose lives we touch.

It seems to me that nothing could be further from the example of Jesus Christ. Jesus willingly took the mockery, the insults, the spit. He quietly endured nails through His hands, being hung publicly on a criminal's cross, and rejection from heaven and earth. Is that a picture of vulnerability? In the light of His pattern, can I be proud? Once a lady asked me, concerning my testimony about depression, "When did you decide to go public?" Well, I don't remember ever making a clear-cut decision to be open about my story, but being public about what I went through has been a healing experience for me. And though I have much to learn about vulnerability and openness, I believe that when it is practiced in an appropriate way, it is helpful for those who are willing to do it, and for those who see it done.

There were times when God chose to speak to me through poetry. I read anything that seemed to be inspired. When I needed to be reminded of the importance of sheer courage or patience or that suffering often has deep purpose, I turned to "A Psalm of Life" by Henry Wadsworth Longfellow.

Tell me not in mournful numbers,
Life is but an empty dream!—
For the soul is dead that slumbers,
And things are not what they seem.

Life is real! Life is earnest!
And the grave is not its goal;
Dust thou art, to dust returnest,
Was not spoken of the soul.

Not enjoyment, and not sorrow,
Is our destined end or way;
But to act, that each tomorrow
Find us farther than today.

Let us then be up and doing,
With a heart for any fate
Still achieving, still pursuing
Learn to labor and to wait.

The Heavenly Father out of His creative abundance taught me truth through music, books, sermons, articles—a legion of things, and oh, how He used His Word.

I remember well those days when I had to force myself to perform simple daily tasks because I was so exhausted from trying to free myself from the anxiety trap. Time after time the Lord through His Holy Spirit brought to my mind a verse or passage of Scripture: "But those who hope in the Lord will renew their strength. They will soar on wings like eagles; they will run and not grow weary, they will walk and not be faint" (Isa. 40:31). Or when I thought I had lost all ability to go on,

He would remind me: "I can do everything through him who gives me strength" (Phil. 4:13).

During those days when I was paralyzed by fear, I was strengthened by the words from Isaiah 41:10: "So do not fear, for I am with you; do not be dismayed, for I am your God. I will strengthen you and help you; I will uphold you with my righteous right hand."

I've been told that "if "—"but what if?" and "if only"—is the universal cry of the neurotic.

Remember the sad accusation Martha made as she ran out to meet Jesus following the death of Lazarus? "Lord, *if* you had been here, my brother would not have died" (John 11:21, italics mine).

Routinely I called out, "Lord, if . . . " Then one day God gave me an "if," and it changed the course of my praying. I was reading in the Book of James when the fifth verse of chapter one snagged my attention: "*If* any of you lacks wisdom, he should ask God, who gives generously to all without finding fault, and it will be given to him" (italics mine). New meaning gushed from that verse! What a promise. God knew about my quest. I shot up a simple prayer, "Now, God, You said that. It is Your explicit promise, and I intend to claim it."

And I did. Though I felt no immediate relief, God and I both knew that we had made a transaction in that verse. In the sleepless nighttime I would give those words back to God and state my case: "Lord, I need wisdom from you so I can understand and overcome my anxieties." Then I would wait and trust. Sometimes I would just wait—trusting was too hard.

As the perpetual winds of time blew over the pages of my calendar, insights came. They came slowly, sometimes painfully, but they came.

In this day and age when hundreds of helpful books are available to those who suffer mentally, it is hard to believe that thirty years ago there was almost nothing, especially for the Christian. Conservative Christians were afraid of psychiatry, perhaps because Freud was critical of religion, seeing it as a "mass neurosis." And early leaders in the field of pastoral counseling were very theologically liberal.

In those dark days my father-in-law providentially gave us a copy of *The Power of Positive Thinking* by Dr. Norman Vincent Peale. I have never heard Dr. Peale speak, and I'm not familiar with his ministry. Let me quickly say that I do not believe in the current trend of belief that leaves out God and promotes the idea that if we think it long enough and strong enough it will happen. Neither do I believe in the "name it, claim it" philosophy. Thirty-seven years ago, however, Dr. Peale put some godly ideas in that little book that helped me. With faltering faith I read and re-read the passages that emphasized the power of God and its availability to me.

I was encouraged with the assurance that I could find a way out: "I caution you not to take the attitude that you are in a situation in which nobody has been before. There is no such situation. Practically speaking there are only a few human stories, and they have all been enacted previously. This is a fact that you must never forget—there are people who have overcome every conceivable difficult situation, even the one in which you now find yourself and which to you seems utterly hopeless. So did it seem to some others, but they found a way up, a path over, a pass through."

I would read those words, then pull Janie and Becky up on my lap and through gritted teeth I would vow anew, "If there is any way—if there is any way to beat this, I'll find it. If others have, so can I. I'll do it for you. I'll do it for myself."

Another powerful insight was made clear to me on one of those days when I felt harassed as a mother. I was having a terrible time with my homemaking chores, and the children couldn't seem to get along. Frightening, obsessive thoughts so bombarded me that I became concerned that I would hurt the girls some way. Finally I worked myself into a petrified state, and as I hit a crescendo, I telephoned Grover at work. "Grover,

I can't stay with the children by myself; I'm too scared. You'll have to come home." For several minutes I complained into the phone, trying to describe the impasse to which I had come. When I finally paused for a response, I heard a deliberate and surprising reply.

"Martha, I have a job to do here. I am trying to do it to the best of my ability, and I cannot come home. You have a job to do there," he continued. "Now hang up the phone and get with it."

How could he say that to me? But it was a moment of truth. Whether he understood the problem and was responding with real discernment, I seriously doubt, but what he said proved to be therapeutic. I knew in that instant that he believed I was able to look after our children, and it restored some of my confidence. Even though I was suffering, I was still a responsible person. It was a small step toward the realization that I could practice at least a degree of anxiety tolerance, and, more important, I did not have to be afraid of fear.

My doctor had previously commented that my concern over the fear was a large part of the problem. Back then it was difficult for me to comprehend, but it did open up some understanding of the fact that fear is only a symptom, and if I can be objective about the fear feeling and not become involved with it, I can avoid compounding it, and thus eliminate some of the suffering.

In my quest for insight into my mental suffering, I needed to learn that recovery is a process. I had to put away my expectations for instantaneous results.

Whenever I read the gospel account of Lazarus's illness and death and Jesus' response to Mary and Martha, it always struck me that although Jesus was very fond of them, when Mary and Martha sent word to Him that Lazarus was sick, He stayed where He was for two days and made no move to go to them.

For a long time I felt that though I called on Jesus, He made no move toward me. No Holy Presence came to lighten the burden or bring healing. My "two days" became eleven years! For eleven years I wandered along the backside of my emotional desert waiting for Jesus to give me fuller understanding, unquestionable assurance, and the peace that passes understanding.

During those desert days there were good times and bad. There were opportunities for varied service with family, church, and community. Even though the relentless anxiety came and went in varying degrees of intensity, I was active and productive. I did some speaking, taught Bible Study, presided at PTA, and was usually the mother who rode the broom through the elementary school on Halloween, for my personality went on. Only those who knew me best realized I had a problem. But I did, and eventually it caught up with me again.

"There are Two of Us Now"

I lay in bed staring at the darkness—hopeless. For weeks I had been unable to eat or sleep, and I was gripped with the fierceness of my neurosis. This time I knew I was not going to be better by myself.

"Grover," my voice cut into the night, "will you call Bob tomorrow and tell him I need to see somebody right away? Either he can help me or he will know someone who can."

The availability of psychiatric help in our area had increased in the years since my hospitalization. And a most remarkable thing had happened: Grover's younger brother, Bob, had become Bob R. Maughon, M.D. We had a bona fide psychiatrist right in our own family! Again my loving Father provided abundantly and kept His promise, "If any of you lacks wisdom . . . ask of God . . . and it will be given . . . " (James 1:5).

I had been reluctant to see Bob professionally because my most vivid impression of him was the fun-loving, clown-around, little brother—the college kid wearing dirty white bucks and borrowed ties, which he usually forgot to return. But my back was against the wall. I had to get professional help, and I had to quit putting it off.

After carefully considering the advisability of treating a relative, Bob decided to take me on. My first patient-to-doctor conversation with him was by telephone. After letting me vent my noxious emotions, he quietly responded, "Remember, you are no longer alone in this—there are two of us now."

His words were comforting and remedial as they soaked into my mind, and encouragement began to trickle through my thoughts.

My psychotherapy began immediately. We would get our families together for visits, and Bob and I would go aside, often in the backyard, for my sessions. We called it my backyard therapy. It was remarkable—more helpful than I ever imagined. Therapy and healing fell everywhere.

One spring morning while we were relaxing under the shade trees, I began to tell Bob about the night Becky was born. I didn't know why I wanted to tell him this, but as the incident and all of its ramifications were unfolding once again, I began to cry. The warm tears surged down my face in such profusion, I became embarrassed.

"I don't know why I am crying," I apologized. "It was all so long ago."

"You are crying because it hurts," was Bob's gentle reply.

How could it hurt after all those years? What had I felt that had cut so deeply?

As I reviewed the events involved in Becky's birth, I began to realize what powerful feelings of rejection surfaced from that experience. I felt that I had been a failure and had brought disappointment and embarrassment to my loved ones.

I had thought my doctor was angry with me for calling the ambulance instead of going on to the hospital. In the race to the hospital we had slowed down by the fire department in response to an "Emergency" sign they had posted on the main highway, but the fire department didn't want to get involved. I felt that the filling station attendant wanted the earth to open up and swallow him . . . or better still, swallow us. I felt that loved ones were embarrassed because I had given birth to the baby in public. I thought I had hurt and worried them. I felt that Grover was disappointed that I had not presented him with a boy, although he did not say anything then nor has he ever said or done anything that would justify that feeling.

Then there followed all the adverse events while I was in the hospital, including the separation from Becky, and the seeming unconcern that prevailed when I tried to tell them I was in trouble. Then, when I was ready to be discharged, the hospital didn't want to give Becky a birth certificate because she had been born outside of the hospital.

In therapy, Bob helped me to understand that there is a definite connection between our hurts and our anger. Hurts can set off emotions that ultimately bring about anxiety and/or depression. When we hurt, anger follows, eventually if not immediately.

Gary Collins also discusses the relationship of hurts and anger. "Perhaps most anger begins when we feel hurt, because of a disappointment or because of the actions of some other person. Instead of admitting the hurt, people mull over it, ponder what happened, and begin to get angry. The anger then builds and becomes so strong that it hides the hurt. If the anger is not admitted and expressed and dealt with, it then leads to revenge. This involves thoughts of hurting another person— either the one who caused the original hurt, or someone else who is nearby.

"Revenge sometimes leads to destructive, violent actions, but this can get us into trouble, and violence is not acceptable, especially for a Christian. As a result, some people try to hide their feelings. This takes energy which wears down the body so that the emotions eventually come to the surface in the form of psychosomatic symptoms. Others, consciously or unconsciously, condemn themselves for their attitudes and become depressed as a result."

We don't like to admit to ourselves or to others that we are angry when someone hurts us, rejects us, or forces us into a situation we don't want to be in. As Christians we will call it anything but anger. We say we are hurt, disappointed, upset, perplexed—anything but angry.

But the truth is we are angry, and it is normal. When we refuse to identify and deal with the anger, it usually goes underground, and that is when it gives us trouble. It speaks to us from our unconscious mind and causes varying types of negative feelings.

Dr. M. Scott Peck in *The Road Less Traveled* discusses the importance of our learning to deal appropriately with anger, learning the right time to express anger and the right time not to express anger. "To handle our anger with full adequacy and competence, an elaborate, flexible response system is required. It is no wonder then, that to learn to handle our anger is a complex task which usually cannot be completed before adulthood, or even mid-life, and which often is never completed."

If we want to enjoy good emotional and mental health, we must get on with the business of learning about our anger patterns—how to call it what it is, how to get it out into the open, how to talk with God about it and let Him begin the healing. Paul said, "Do not let the sun go down while you are still angry" (Eph. 4:26). He did not say this because all anger is wrong, but because unresolved, seething hostility will cause us serious problems, even illness. God wants the very best for us; and our rebellion, conscious or unconscious, warranted or unwarranted, blocks His best in our lives.

2

LOW SELF-WORTH

A Root Problem

W hat I experienced at the time of Becky's birth did result in a hurt that ultimately led to anxiety, but that was only a small part of the picture. As I continued to share both my feelings and experiences with Bob, we dredged up other destructive patterns in my life.

I began to realize that I didn't think very much of myself. I was always afraid I would fail to measure up to people's expectations of me.

Once in my dialogue with Bob I made a reference to Grover.

"Well," Bob mused, "I wondered when you were going to get around to him."

I was surprised. "Does he have something to do with this?"

"He is your life" was the succinct reply.

Strangely, I had always thought that I just had an affliction of some kind. I didn't know that my illness could be caused in a great measure by what was going on in my life every day. That makes me seem a little dense, I guess, but apparently it is a common occurrence; for in recent years I have counseled with a number of anxious, depressed people who were dealing furiously with their feelings yet had hardly taken into account what was going on between them and those with whom they related day by day. Even though learning about our past may help show us behavior patterns and help us understand reasons behind our feelings, we still have to get honest with ourselves about what is going on in our present relationships.

In my case, because of the way I saw myself I felt threatened by certain people and situations. Because I didn't like myself, I felt that Grover didn't love me; this was causing me to read all kinds of negative messages into things he did and said.

He was human after all and he didn't always do and say the right things. As I began to realize that I felt inferior to my husband, I also realized that I felt inferior to a lot of people and could be made to feel inferior to anybody. I had never come to grips with my inferiority complex. In fact, I had coped with my insecurities by developing a rather gregarious personality, and I thought it was impossible that one so outgoing could be basically insecure. Of course my overtness was a manifestation of my fear that I would not be accepted.

We Must Learn to Suffer

Interestingly, now I can often identify even blatantly aggressive behavior that stems from psychological problems. Some of us are turned inward and find hostility toward others difficult to express. But others of us turn our anger outward. I was told that both types of personalities will many times live out their lives with crippling neuroses because they would rather feel the pain of neurosis than face the problem and endure the pain of delving into themselves looking for truth. They cling to old, safe behaviorisms fearing reality and the suffering that might accompany change. I did not want that to happen to me.

Dr. M. Scott Peck says, "Life is a series of problems. . . . We attempt to skirt around problems rather than meet them head on. . . . This tendency to avoid problems and emotional suffering inherent in them is the primary basis of all mental illness." We must learn how to experience legitimate suffering lest we fail to grow.

And Carl Jung's statement that "Neurosis is always a substitute for legitimate suffering" concurs with Dr. Peck's position.

We Don't Develop Overnight

My therapy rolled on, hammering out some rough places. Bob was helping me to recognize my unhealthy thinking and helping me begin to believe in my own worth. He encouraged me to look at my negative self and to deal with the low self-esteem problem that we had identified as a serious contributor to my emotional illness.

I was learning some important principles: Most authorities agree that our self-evaluation is a result of the way we were treated and/or taught in the early years of our lives. Jo Berry in *Can You Love Yourself?* asserts, "You don't develop as a person overnight but are a composite of all the bits and pieces of trivia and trauma you've lived through since your birth."

When a child receives negative messages, verbal or non-verbal, and is not assured of favor, he or she falls into a rather pathetic routine of seeking it. Hurts that are programmed into a sensitive child seem to smolder and flair up in later life. Growing up, I always felt inferior to my two brothers. I remember when an older cousin used to visit us. He would invite the boys to go to a movie with him. When I would ask to go too, he would say, "We don't want any little ole girls tagging along." It seemed that the first thing I did wrong was to be a girl.

Perhaps one of the most subtle but frequent offenses is conditional love. That is, putting forward the idea, "I will love you if " and "people won't like you if." These principles stated or implied cause us to grow up convinced that we are loved only when we earn it, when we behave according to what significant others expect of us. If we feel that we fall short of what we interpret as the expectations of those others, we feel unlovable; therefore unloved.

Even in adulthood if we are constantly subjected to criticism or faultfinding by key people, we tend to devaluate ourselves and suffer feelings of inadequacy . . . or failing to make it.

Each of us has a perception of who we are and a perception of who we ought to be. The greater the gap between the two, the more room there is for insecurity and low self-esteem. But it is important for us to realize that our idealized self can be extremely unrealistic and inappropriate. And trying to become that self is demanding and sometimes counterproductive.

As we seek to close that gap between goals and achievement, some of us develop a life-style of striving and feeling failure. I became acutely aware of this when a man I once worked for told me that I hated to be wrong worse than anybody he had ever seen. The need to be right may be one indication of poor self-esteem. Other manifestations might be the habit of criticizing others, a drive to win badges and awards, running with the "best" people, bragging, a compulsion to make a lot of money—any of a number of things that we are driven to do.

On the other hand, some practice a sort of pseudo humility, a self-abasement. They live a life of admitted failure because that is easier than trying to succeed.

David A. Seamands writes about this in his book, Healing For Damaged Emotions: "The person with low self-esteem is always trying to prove himself. He has a need to be right in every situation, to verify himself. He gets all wrapped up in constantly looking at himself."

And John Powell analyzed his own emotions in *Fully Human, Fully Alive* and gave me this insight: "I found in myself a strong, almost compulsive, need to please others—to meet their expectations. This delusion—that I had to be 'for others' and never 'for myself'—was truly a ring in my nose by which I was being led around. The discovery of the delusion led to a whole explosion of insights about the need to love oneself in balance with loving other people."

We seem to understand the causes of ego destruction, yet with all we have learned in this area, we continue to repeat the problem. We lay on each other the burdens and put-downs that perpetuate the poor image syndrome. For many people, liking and appreciating self is very difficult. For some it is impossible.

Sometimes I have to be reminded that as a Christian I have every reason to see myself as a person of infinite worth. I know that God created me in His own likeness, that He loves me and desires my fellowship. He bought me with the death of His Son and He does not intend for me to think of myself as worthless.

When Jesus said the second greatest commandment is that I should love my neighbor as myself, He was reflecting the fact that healthy regard for self is important. If I dislike myself and then care for others in the same way, they will surely be in trouble.

Of course I am unworthy of God's great love and His sacrifice of Christ on the cross, but that does not mean that I am worthless. If God had considered me worthless, there would have been no Calvary. Christ's death proves my worth, not my lack of it.

As I thought of the magnitude of that truth, these words fell from my heart.

> *Kneeling at the cross*
> *   I am unworthy.*
> *I claim the righteousness*
> *   of the Son.*
> *Clothed in Him*
> *   I am complete, pure, clean*
> *   I am good,*

> A royal child of the King, am I
> An heir to all He owns.
> Glory, splendor
> they are mine
> and yet,
>
> I am unworthy
> kneeling at the cross.

One day in therapy the conversation between Bob and me turned to Janie's behavior. I sighed, "Well, we surely don't want her to turn out like me." Bob looked at me deliberately. With approval in his voice he said, "I pray she will be like you." A warm tide of affirmation washed over me as I heard this profound endorsement. A doctor, for whom I had great respect, was telling me that my daughter could be like me and still be okay! And he knew me. He was my brother-in-law. I needed this kind of affirmation, and this incident was a turning point in my healing.

"Set Her Free"

Years ago my beautiful friend Eve used to pray with me when I would be tyrannized by symptoms of worthlessness. I remember she used to pray, "Lord, just set her free." And I would think, "That's right, Lord, I need to be set free."

In His own time and way He answered Eva's prayer. Though there remained many things yet to be learned, the therapy I received from Bob literally gave me back my life. The once persistent cloud of anxiety was dissolved, and I was again able to enjoy life fully. I could see new horizons and plan for my future. I no longer was plagued by the futility that had been my constant companion.

I was able to finish my poem:

Who knows the dark tormentor?
   That one who wrecks the plans of man
   And slays the joys of life
   Who stalks his prey throughout the day
   And hovers in the night.
He sits heavy on my chest
   Relentless,
      Robbing,
         Mocking me.
His name is Fear
   And I know him well.

Who knows the One who conquers fear?
   Beloved One
   Who gives Himself
      in peace and light
   Jesus Christ, Holy God, Comforter
   I know Him too—
And He knows me.

As I rejoiced in this new measure of emotional health, Psalm 40:2 had a special meaning for me: "He lifted me out of the pit of despair, out from the bog and mire, and set my feet on a hard, firm path and steadied me as I walked along" (LB). And the song of my heart became, "I will tell of the loving-kindnesses of God. I will praise him for all he has done; I will rejoice in his great goodness" (Isa. 63:7 LB).

I claimed as a personal promise the verse, "I will instruct you (says the Lord) and guide you along the best pathway for your life; I will advise you and watch your progress" (Ps. 32:8 LB). How I counted on God's advice, though that advice might not always be what I had hoped for or come when I thought it should. And I was grateful that He watched my progress. I had to keep reminding myself that my life was a process and that emotional maturation was a process too.

Feeling good about ourselves can be more than just a goal. We can find answers: spiritual, psychological, and physical answers.

"If any man lack wisdom let him ask. . . ." I had asked, and He had answered.

And there was more.

3

GUILT

Bound to Inferiority

The smell of hot barbecue, frying pork skins, corn on the cob, and peanuts boiling in the black iron pot filled the air and joined with the sound of country music and the blacksmith's anvil to form a backdrop for the Cotton Pickin' Fair.

Mother and I were shuffling leisurely from booth to booth palming and inspecting the varied handwork that had come to the little town of Gay, Georgia. This is one of the best arts and crafts festivals held in our area, and for some time Mother had wanted me to take her to see it.

I had set a slow pace for the day because Mother was fragile, and I was not sure how much strength she had for this kind of outing. And she did so want to see everything.

The morning slid by, and early afternoon ushered in a close-to-earth autumn sun that beat hot on our heads. Although she didn't complain, with the passing of the hours, Mother's strength and enthusiasm seemed to be waning. When I asked how she felt, she mentioned a pain high in her back and a feeling of weakness. I was too far from my car to start home, so I quickly led her to a nearby bench and sat her down. She didn't look well, and I asked again, "How are you feeling now?" and feebly she replied, "I can't see."

It suddenly occurred to me that she was slipping into unconsciousness. In the midst of thousands of people I was alone and frightened. I turned to a gentleman sitting next to me on the bench. "Will you please help me? My mother is ill. Please just watch her for a minute while I look for the rescue squad." On hearing my request, the man silently shifted his position on the bench so that his back was directly toward Mother and me.

By this time Mother could hardly respond, so I left her and fled out into the crowd. I prayed and ran for only a few yards before I spotted the Emergency Medical Technicians. They reacted quickly, called for the ambulance, and went to Mother. As we waited for the stretcher, I anxiously patted her hands and her face. I kept telling her to hang on. Just before they put her in the ambulance, I told her I loved her. With eyes closed and with a weak voice, she echoed my words, "I love you."

I glanced back at the bench. The man who was unwilling to help us had disappeared.

As the stretcher was shoved into the ambulance, I was numb. I thought my mother was dying. The medical technician who drove the ambulance seemed to think so too. When he pulled himself into the cab where I was sitting, he reported that her vital signs were extremely poor and that he would not risk going all the way to Atlanta.

As the ambulance whipped along the narrow county road, all kinds of memories and thoughts raced through my mind. I pictured how excited Mother had looked that morning as she waited for the festival gate to open. How eager she had been to find little gifts for friends and family. And how pleased she was when I let her buy me some corn shuck flowers.

All of a sudden my anxiety reached a desperate pitch, and I knew I couldn't stand it if she died.

I watched through the cab window as the female EMT administered intravenous fluids. Finally the technician looked up at me, smiled, and made a circle with her thumb and index finger as a sign that Mother was responding. I felt a little relieved.

As strange as it seemed to me and to both medical technicians, by the time we reached the hospital, Mother had completely rallied. When the doctor checked her, she had completely recovered. The only thing the doctor could determine was that she had simply fainted.

It was incomprehensible.

For days after that ordeal I was anxious and depressed. True, it had been a frightening experience, but my reaction was out of proportion. There seemed to be something more involved than just my response to a scary episode. I couldn't settle down. No matter how I thought of Mother, I felt I was mistreating her. I was overcome with guilt. My anxiety level kept climbing.

About the time I decided that somebody was going to have to throw me a rope, Bob dropped in for a visit.

It was on a Sunday afternoon, and, as usual, the Atlanta Falcons were playing football in our den. Bob and Grover were captivated by the game, but between plays and at halftime I doggedly inserted my lamentations and questions concerning my emotional state.

Later, when I got Bob's full attention, our talk helped me understand why I was feeling what I was, and our discussion ignited some important growth for me.

It occurred to me that the mother-daughter tie is a most tender relationship. For some reason, related at least in part to my childhood, I was in a double bind with my mother. Without meaning to she could send me on a "guilt trip" with just a sentence or a look or even nothing.

This is in no way intended to be a disparagement of my mother. She is an excellent person and has always been a good, loving, caring parent. But as an adult I was more sensitive to her disapproval than I should have been. I simply had not grown up in the area of the mother-daughter relationship, and my feelings of guilt and remorse were exaggerated and inappropriate.

As I began to face the truth and deal with it, I knew that one guilt-producing factor in the relationship was that I had moved away from the town where she lived. She had not really wanted me to move. The decision had been a careful, prayerful one for Grover and me, but later I was not sure I should have put thirty miles between mother and me, since she was living alone and getting older. Because the feelings resulting from my guilt were so intense, I decided I would take a direct approach and talk to her about it. She listened and actually was quite surprised that I was having to deal with so much guilt where she was concerned. She told me that she loved me very much and didn't want to do or say anything that would result in pain for me and this included my painful guilt reaction. I was able to accept this as her true feeling. She was pleased when I felt good. As a result of this new point of view, I was able to shake much of the debilitating guilt.

Since that time my mother has had a very serious illness and she is still far from well. I had the heartbreaking responsibility of uprooting her from the home she loved, relocating her in my own home and assuming the responsibility for her care. This is a role that neither of us wanted me to have and it has been a difficult adjustment for both of us. Now I realize why God let me experience that terrible day at the arts and crafts festival and the miserable days that followed, for I could have never done what I had to for mother if I had stayed on the guilt trip.

Inferiority and Guilt—Non-Identical Twins

In my quest to understand my feelings of guilt, I read several books that gave me insight into the interrelationship of guilt and inferiority.

John Powell, in his book *Why Am I Afraid To Tell You Who I Am?* calls inferiority and guilt non-identical twins. He explains that while inferiority results from the conflict between what one actually is and what one would like to be, guilt arises out of the conflict between what one actually does or feels and what one thinks one should do or feel.

This is exactly what my life experience had been. There was a gap between what I wanted to be for my mother and others and what I felt I was.

Powell further explains: "In inferiority feelings, there is a recognition of weakness and inadequacy. . . . People who suffer from inferiority feelings . . . seek to eradicate their feelings . . . by showing superiority in some form of rivalry. . . . Guilt feelings on the contrary can be verbalized: 'I'm not much good. Most of what I want to do . . . and have done . . . seems mean and evil. I really deserve contempt and punishment for my failures. . . .' "

It seems that all feelings of inferiority are accompanied by the thought, "I am bad. I should do better." Because of this, it is impossible to separate guilt and low self-worth. My situation as a child was typical of most of us. I had a happy childhood, but I was brought up by humans, and I am sure mistakes were made. I was a sensitive child, and somewhere along the way I set up for myself an unrealistic standard of behavior. I developed an overly sensitive conscience, a strong sense of self-blame and guilt.

Once when I was a little girl—not old enough to go to school—my parents took me to see Santa Claus. As I approached the huge chair where he sat, I looked in wide-eyed awe at the great Father Christmas. He took me on his lap, and after the usual "Ho-Ho-Ho," he stabbed me with the traditional zinger, "Have you been a good little girl this year?"

"Oh, no sir," I replied, afraid if I told him I had been good, he would know I was lying, and that would compound my transgression.

"Well, you haven't been very bad, have you?" insisted a bewildered Santa, trying to salvage me.

"Yes, sir, I have," continued my confession. I guess I have always thought of myself as a bad girl.

Dr. James Dobson makes a profound statement concerning self-blame: "Hospitals for the emotionally disturbed are filled with . . . patients who have been unable to meet their own expectations and are now broken with self-blame and even personal hatred."

Sometimes in guilt we will feel the need of punishment and will even seek to punish ourselves. Plato said, "The soul will run eagerly to its judge." This need for punishment may result in any number of problems such as physical illness, hostility, anxiety, depression, or a combination of these.

True Guilt or False Guilt?

As I continued to research the guilt concept, I saw that guilt involves a very wide and varied expanse including legal guilt (breaking civil laws), social guilt (breaking social rules), personal guilt (violation of our consciences), and theological guilt (breaking God's law).

I also realized that there was a difference between real guilt and imagined or neurotic guilt. All of us suffer pangs of guilt at times, especially when we have violated "the laws," and guilt is not always bad. It can motivate us to healthy living and the helping of other people. However, when we are just going around in circles with our guilt, when there is absolutely nothing that can be done about it, when we have turned it over to the Lord and the burden of guilt is still with us, we can assume that it is false or neurotic.

Although some psychiatrists and psychologists do not believe in theological guilt, as a Christian I am convinced that there is a very valid and proper place for this kind of guilt in our lives. We are truly guilty when we are breaking God's laws or when we are living in opposition to the teachings of Jesus or when we behave in a way that hurts others. As we become pricked in our consciences, we need to repent, receive God's forgiveness, and change our behavior. It is to our mental, emotional, and spiritual benefit to live in the light of the revelation of Jesus Christ.

A very real difficulty arises, however, when a Christian seeks to follow a self-incriminating conscience that is not inspired by God. A tender conscience can even be the work of Satan, for he is described in the Scripture as the "accuser of the brethren," and he often brings torment to the sensitive soul who, perhaps more than most others, is trying to live a good Christian life.

Dr. James Mallory in Untwisted Living shed some light on that issue for me. "I would warn against assuming that guilt always comes from breaking some biblical law. It is not that simple. Many people are eaten up with guilt, not because they have broken some law and won't repent, but because of other problems. . . ."

I am grateful that in my search to learn causes for the inferiority and guilt in my life, the Lord provided counselors who helped me learn to discern between true guilt and false guilt, and to make a start toward straightening out my warped pattern of neurotic, false guilt.

Perfectionism—A Neurotic Syndrome

Unfortunately when we are caught up in neurotic or false guilt and are striving to attain our standards of "ought to" and "ought not to," we fall into the pattern of perfectionism.

David Seamands says that, "Perfectionism is the most disturbing emotional problem among evangelical Christians. It walks into my office more often than any other single hang-up."

And he also explains the difference between true Christian perfection (to which we are called) and perfectionism:

"Perfectionism is a counterfeit for Christian perfection, holiness, sanctification, or the Spirit-filled life. Instead of making us holy persons and integrated personalities—that is, whole persons in Christ—perfectionism leaves us spiritual Pharisees and emotional neurotics.

"Immature and sensitive believers can become neurotic perfectionists who are guilt-ridden, tight-haloed, unhappy, and uncomfortable."

In perfectionism we become legalistic, burdened, and usually judgmental. Often we become angry, consciously or unconsciously, and part of our anger is directed toward God whom we believe we can never satisfy, no matter how hard we may try.

Seamands describes the experience of the perfectionist: "Under the stress and strain of trying to live with a self he can't like, a God he can't love, and other people he can't get along with, the strain can become too much."

Certainly there are no Christians who behave perfectly. Our righteousness is as "filthy rags." The saints are simply those of us who have received Christ, put our faith in the healing, cleansing power of His blood, and stand before God without blame because God sees us through Jesus.

Our perfection, then, is His gift to us—not our gift to Him.

Toward Healing

There are three specific concepts that helped me with my own guilt complex:

First, I learned to see myself as a totally guilty person, not as a person doing things that were wrong. I learned that the point is not that I "do" wrong things but that I "am" guilty. No matter what I do, I am still guilty compared to the standards Christ set. I am never going to get it right, and that is exactly why Jesus died. God in Jesus Christ said, "Yes, you are guilty, you failed yourself, others, and Me. But I love you anyway."

I have the loving favor of God, not because I earned it, but because Jesus earned it for me. There is absolutely no way I can build a merit system, much less live up to it.

Elementary? You'd be surprised how many people have difficulty getting that truth to walk around in their lives!

The second concept comes from the writings of David Seamands. In order to please God, I must forgive myself. God has told us that if we are to receive His forgiveness, we must be willing to forgive the wrongs that people do, and that includes forgiving myself. This is a tremendous truth for those of us who have neurotic guilt. I've had a wonderful time learning to forgive myself—I am under God's command to do that.

Third, I was relieved when I learned the difference between constructive sorrow and neurotic guilt. When I make mistakes now, or when I fail in some way, I am truly sorry, and I seek God's forgiveness and try to make restitution wherever I can. But I no longer feel that I should remain in bondage or destroy myself. I am able to accept 1 John 1:9, "If we confess our sins he is faithful and just and will forgive us our sins and purify us from all unrighteousness." As I repent, I can pray, "Yes Lord, I agree with you, what I did was sinful. Thank you for forgiving and forgetting the wrong."

I have come to realize that I do not serve God or anybody else when I wallow in guilt and self-condemnation. The Scripture reminds us that, "Therefore, there is now no condemnation for those who are in Christ Jesus" (Rom. 8:1). God does not sanction the continual harassing of myself over coming up short. On the contrary, Christ paid a very high price to spare me that.

As I considered the destructive power of guilt in our lives and realized the tremendous impact we have on each other in the establishing of guilt complexes, especially in the child-parent relationship, I became eager to do what I could to spare my daughters any pressure that would result in problems for them.

I am sure that at times I have put a burden of high expectations on them, as I hoped for their achievements scholastically, socially, vocationally, and spiritually. But as I think of our tender mother-daughter relationships, I am trying to set them free so they can grow and choose their own direction according to their mature, healthy, divinely guided consciences. I want them to be emotionally independent of me and happy in their decisions, with no backlash of inappropriate guilt. What we did in earlier years can't be undone, but God is a redeemer who can take our mistakes and work them for good in the lives of these loved ones.

Not long ago I embroidered a sampler for each of the girls, and the sentiment I cross-stitched there was: "Always a daughter, now too my friend."

Proverbs says, "A friend loves at all times" (Prov. 17:17).

If I could leave my daughters but one legacy, it would be that they know my heart, that they hear me as in unconditional acceptance I declare, "Yes, dear ones, I love you—all the time."

4

SPIRITUAL HEALING

A Gift of God

In the gospel account of Lazarus's death, we find Jesus and Martha at the tomb where Lazarus's dead body had been placed. Jesus called to the men who were standing around and ordered them to take away the stone that sealed the entrance to the tomb.

Martha in her usual pragmatic style was advising Jesus. "Lord, He's been dead four days. If you open that tomb, folks will be able to smell him all the way to Jerusalem" (my own paraphrase).

But Martha's remarks betrayed her lack of knowledge of the power and intent of her Lord. I cherish His response: "Did I not tell you that if you believed, you would see the glory of God?" (John 11:40).

Many times I, too, have given advice to Jesus, telling Him how I thought He ought to run His business. But in spite of my agitation and poor understanding of His purpose, He is giving me a glimpse of the glory of God.

A very real contribution to my ability to see God was made by therapy I received under Dr. James D. Mallory, Christian psychiatrist and director of the Atlanta Counseling Center.

My therapy under Bob had restored me, and I maintained a level of emotional equilibrium. Sometimes, however, I was thwarted by some unsettled spiritual issues. When I learned that Dr. Mallory was practicing in Atlanta, I was strongly impressed to see him. I believed that one who is committed to Christ and His teachings and is at the same time trained in the science of the mind and emotions is in the strongest possible position to bring healing to anxious and depressed persons. Dr. Mallory is one of many available counselors who have these qualifications, and he has made an enduring contribution to my quest for healthy, abundant living.

In our first interview Dr. Mallory described my spiritual insecurity as a "hanger on" to my deeper problem of poor self-esteem. "You feel that you are unacceptable to yourself, unacceptable to your husband, and unacceptable to God," he said, explaining the sequence of my emotional activity.

For years I had envisioned myself going out into eternity, stretching my hand up to meet God's. Just as our hands were almost close enough to touch, I would stub my toe. I could never quite make it. In the final analysis He would not have me. This is not what I reasoned; it is what I felt. And I felt it with all of the torment that a Christian can know if he or she feels separated from God.

I had heard the Scripture from childhood: "For God so loved the world that he gave his only begotten Son, that *whosoever* believeth in him should not perish, but have everlasting life" (John 3:16 KJV) (italics mine).

As a young girl I had memorized, "Believe on the Lord Jesus Christ, and thou shalt be saved" (Acts 16:31 KJV).

I knew that salvation was a gift from God, freely given to anyone who would receive Jesus Christ by faith and commit one's life to Him. I believed that, but somehow I felt that it was for everybody but me. I didn't understand how I could be an exception, but there persisted a stubborn futility concerning God's willingness to accept me.

Just Give It to God

Once I attended a seminar in which there was great emphasis on the concept of giving our problems to God. "Oh boy, this is great," I thought. And I couldn't wait to have a problem so I could try it. I didn't have to wait very long. Soon my old problems of feeling very guilty and burdened because I was not all God wanted me to be came pushing in. I prayed very carefully and deliberately; I confessed my sin and asked forgiveness. And then I gave it to God. There was just one problem; after I gave it to Him, I still had it. I was then more disturbed and depressed than ever, for I was faced with the failure of having done it wrong. I couldn't even give my problems to God the way other people did—He wouldn't have them.

Dr. Mallory explained that the ability to give a matter to God and be rid of the anxiety of it altogether can have as much or more to do with psychological factors as with faith. People who are healthy psychologically are a lot better at this than those of us who are already struggling for relief from problems that have been collecting through the years.

This is not to say that we should give up praying and trusting God for answers, but we must recognize that people have varying abilities to enjoy relief from worry and harassment. I still give my problems to God, ask Him to be with me in them, and seek to rest in Him, but I have a healthier understanding of what is involved in that. There is just no guarantee of instant freedom from predicaments.

As I gained another degree of spiritual maturity, I began to see my spirituality in a very different light. You might say I am a member of the UTBASS Club. That is the "Used To Be A Super Saint Club." For years I tried to fly with those who count themselves as more spiritual, more "into the Word" than most other Christians. I was afraid to allow my real self to be known, lest others would think less of my spirituality. Living under these high expectations brings a great deal of pressure, and those who try to present the constant victorious picture often end up depressed.

Stanley E. Lindquist, in an article entitled "Dishonesty on Cloud Nine" from *Christianity Today*, discusses the necessity of eliminating emotional dishonesty among Christians. He reasons that if he made the mistake of comparing his state at its low and horrible times to the exaltation described in testimonies that often suggest that the "spiritual high" is the Christian's continual state, he would be tempted to give up on everything. Most Christians, however, don't have the opportunity that he as a counselor has to see both sides of the coin. Most Christians do not see those "victorious" people when they come for counseling to face honestly the low points of their lives.

The result, then, of this emotional dishonesty among Christians is that the disturbed Christian who makes a Herculean effort to reach those "spiritual high" places often falls into deep, lonely despair that may lead to neurosis, psychosis, or even suicide.

Dr. Mallory taught me that my endeavor to be the super Christian was a very common malady, especially among evangelical Christians. Failing to do and think the right thing all the time and then being depressed over the failure is a common problem.

"When you give up the philosophy of perfection in this neurotic sense," Dr. Mallory explained in a counseling session, "you may think you are taking second-best Christianity, but you are not. Being real, being honest about your pain, making allowances for your humanity, learning to drop some of the nonessential 'oughts' and 'shoulds'—this is where the growth is."

This has proven to be very true and very liberating. My spiritual maturity was hung up on my efforts. But when I allowed myself to turn loose the old ideas, instead of falling into the black abyss the way I thought I would, I sprang free—more free than I had been for a long time. I was free to get to know God better, free to enjoy His grace, free to understand other people—free to be.

I was growing again!

My Christian therapy also enabled me to face the reality of Satan in the world. If you want to scare neurotic people, wait until they are really anxious and then tell them it's Satan. It will probably make them feel possessed by Satan, and it will surely make them more anxious. The first time somebody told me my depression was Satanic, I felt covered up with evil, and my anxiety shot up and stayed elevated for days.

Nevertheless Satan is real and alive, and he is stalking the earth. He invades the thoughts and minds of all of us, and melancholic Christians must be his favorite prey. His goal is to defeat us and destroy our confidence in Christ. He delights to render us useless in the matter of Christian witnessing. He steals our joy.

I needed help to discover Satan's role in my mental suffering. Dr. Mallory's book *Untwisted Living* gave me this insight: "There is a valid sense in which both God and Satan are involved in every circumstance of suffering. If you are at the crossroads, Satan will try to get you to lie, make false accusations, dodge the real issue. He will especially try to get you to focus on the problems that seem overwhelming and trap you in hopelessness. There is also the will, the power, the desire, and the trust of God to see you through the suffering so that you emerge a stronger, healthier, and more whole and fulfilled person."

Therefore we must learn to discern between the guidance God is seeking to give us and the fear and havoc Satan would lay on us. God leads; Satan drives. Satan accuses, but God does not. He gently convicts and leads through His Holy Spirit, the Comforter. "The Counselor, the Holy Spirit . . . will teach you all things. . . . the Spirit of truth . . . will guide you into all truth" (John 14:26; 16:13).

The Scripture teaches that God does not give the spirit of fear, but He gives the spirit of a sound mind (2 Tim. 1:7). A good, healthy conscience comes from the sound thinking and sound interpretations of His Word.

In *Guilt and Freedom*, Bruce Narramore and Bill Counts write, "God is consistent. He doesn't tell us we are significant, forgiven, and disciplined only in love, then whisper in our ears, 'You are a scoundrel; I will punish you. I will pay you back until you repent.' God cannot contradict himself! He doesn't present one message in the Bible and an opposite message by his 'convincing Holy Spirit.' Conviction simply means that God is clearly showing us our sins and admonishing us to change" (p. 124).

Us and Them

Throughout my years of struggles with emotional illness, I have found that sometimes Christians unknowingly do great damage to the emotionally fragile person. Because many Christians have not experienced severe emotional disturbances they do not understand the feelings and reactions such a person might have.

I remember one incident in which the insensitivity of a Christian leader deeply disturbed me. It occurred one Sunday while I was sitting in an adult Sunday school class. I had hurried that day to complete my responsibilities in a youth department so I could hear this particular teacher, for she was reputed to be the best Bible teacher in that church. I slipped into a seat in the back of the room, opened my Bible, and found the place. I don't remember what the lesson was about, but well into the discussion, the teacher remarked, "All we need is just to have faith. If we all had faith, there would be no need for psychiatrists." I couldn't believe she said that!

Later as I complained to God about the way depressed people are constantly subjected to theological interpretations that hurt and undo progress in their lives, He gave me a new truth—my own private concept. It was a little homely but it was something I could hold onto, and it has comforted me many times. It is simply this: There is an "us" and there is a "them." Some people (us) know and understand how a neurotic might think or react in a given situation. We know this either because of our personal experience or because of insight gained in some other way. But there are always with us those (usually the healthy ones) who, through no fault of their own, do not have the foggiest understanding of where we are coming from. They are "them."

I find a lot of "thems" among Christians. Though they mean well and usually are trying to help, they often make sweeping statements and use cliches about faith and trust and how to live the Christian life and about how folks ought to feel. I have had to learn that if Christians say things that cause me fear and confusion, but offer me no sound instruction, it is all right for me to disregard them. For a long time it scared me to filter what respected Christians were saying. I felt as if I were shoving a fist in God's face, but now I can just whisper, "Well, Lord, there's another 'them.' "

I have finally conceded that I cannot expect everyone to understand how I feel in given situations. Yet the cry of my heart is to let folks know that depressives are not mystic or weird, or that we think other people never have stress and strain. It's just that we are dealing with a tendency to become severely depressed, and we have to make allowances for the fear that the stresses we feel might cause us to lose our psychological equilibrium. We feel like we're walking a tightrope sometimes. Most of us have sensitive natures, and we just want our fellow Christians to understand.

A lady once wrote me, "Maybe we could have a Neurotics Anonymous for those of us who have so much trouble with anxiety and depression." Later I learned that this organization is actually already in existence. I think it's a great idea and I wonder if they adopted the helpful motto of Alcoholics Anonymous:

> *God grant me the serenity to accept*
> *the things I cannot change,*
> *The courage to change the things I can*
> *And the wisdom to know the difference.*

Don't Put Me in a Box

Just as it was necessary for me to filter the statements that Christians sometimes made, so I found I occasionally had to filter some of the sermons I was hearing.

For example, there was an excellent, renowned preacher in our area. People came from miles around to hear him. They bought his tapes and played them for hours. He helped hundreds of people. Yet every time I heard this man, I felt as if he had beaten me to the ground with a big stick. I cannot explain it; I just always felt bad after I heard him.

I came to realize that not all ministry was helpful to me. We are not all alike, and we respond differently to different methods. We are diverse creations of a diversified Creator, and our response to what we hear comes from our individual, unique frames of reference. A negative reaction to a message that is helping someone else need not cause me to feel guilty.

This does not mean that God is limited in His ability to reach various types of people. On the contrary, it reflects the amazing limitlessness of God and His unfathomable resources to touch, convict, and minister to all kinds of people.

I also found that not all reading material is helpful to me. Reading has contributed enormously to my growth and understanding, but I have read some books designed to help depressed people that left me more depressed than they found me. I believe this occurs because some writers—though spiritually dynamic—do not have sufficient understanding of depression. It has been good for me to come to the point of being able to evaluate a work and simply throw it over my shoulder if it is not helpful. I no longer feel obligated to try to adjust my thoughts and beliefs when they run counter to those of respected authors. I find the books that help me most, so far as my depression is concerned, are those written by Christian mental health professionals or Christians who understand hurting people and some of their deeply rooted difficulties, including the possibility of biochemical imbalance.

Come to the Party

One of the most significant influences on my spiritual life was made by Karl Olsson. In his book *Come to the Party* Mr. Olsson likens the free, abundant life to a party and reminds us that the Bible is filled with parties, feastings, merriment, and celebrations. The greatest celebration to which we can go is the life lived in Christ Jesus.

Karl Olsson observes humans to be divided into two groups: the blessed and the unblessed—those who feel good about themselves and those who never feel they are making it. And he refers to the well-known story of the prodigal son with its obvious meaning that "God loves us even when we stray from him, and when we mess things up, he not only waits for us but comes running toward us and welcomes us back with a joyous celebration."

There is another meaning to the story. The son who goes away is clearly the blessed son. He is the child who is so secure in his father's love that he is free to claim his inheritance, leave his father, squander the money, mess up his life, return, repent, and accept forgiveness; then he is free to join in the celebration given for him.

The son who stayed at home is the unblessed one—not free to do anything. Though he is always considered the selfish, unforgiving brother, it is easy to see him as one who felt fearful and unaccepted, one who felt he was not pleasing his father. Despite all of his efforts, he had never made it. He never had a party given for him. He is the unblessed one.

And Olsson writes, "The party is in full swing—lights blazing, music blaring, tables laden, singing and dancing, excitement, and joy. The runaway has returned. Outside in the shadows stands a lonely figure looking in, jealous, angry. The older brother. He has never run away. Why has he never had a party?"

Karl Olsson explains in his book that people fall into four categories:

1. those who doubt there is a party
2. those who believe there is a party somewhere, but they're not invited
3. those who believe there is a party, and they're invited, but they don't deserve to stay
4. those who are invited and go and stay.

It took me only a second to know that I fell into the third category. But I have learned, as Mr. Olsson learned, that I can move from the third category to the fourth. I am no less Christian because I have normal feelings of fear, anxiety, doubt, anger, irritation, sensuality, and a host of others. I can cease to push them down under and can face them realistically, ask forgiveness, and receive it.

"Because of Jesus' risking to be human and the price he paid for me, I can risk being human and have freedom to fail. Because Jesus hosted a party in which he himself was bread and wine which he gave the denier and betrayers to eat and drink, I have the courage to come to the party and to be with him and all his blessed and unblessed forever."

Yes, I have discovered that I can be "a child of blessing and belong at the party. And that I need never go away."

After all is said about counseling, teaching, and reading, there remains only one great Authority. Though God made us with differing abilities to understand and assimilate His truth, He guides and watches over us all with the same faithfulness.

As this fact comes alive for me, I see something of His tenderness, His understanding, His forgiveness, His love, His magnificence . . . yes, as Jesus promised Martha . . . I see the glory of God!

5

DEPRESSION
More Than Just a Blue Mood

The old movie titled *Hold Back the Dawn* describes my efforts when the miserable despondency shoves against my mind as I begin to awaken in the early morning hours. I find myself trying to stay asleep in order to escape the dreaded mental state that insists: "Something's wrong, something's wrong, something's wrong."

Even yet, periodically, that red digital "3:00 a.m." gazes back at me countless times. I awaken to wrestle with the "bad feeling" only to find that I cannot go back to sleep.

Sleep disturbance is a classic symptom of depression, and there are many more. Dr. Frank Minirth and Dr. Paul Meier in their book *Happiness Is a Choice* list one hundred and one personality traits of the depressed person. Some of the most typical traits are worry, sadness, feelings of worthlessness and hopelessness, false guilt, anger, fatigue, insomnia, hypochondria, feelings of inferiority, identification problems . . . all the things I've been sharing.

We can see these feelings expressed in this poem written by a struggling teenage girl who was a patient in a state mental hospital. Because she wanted to share her feelings with a friend, she gave this to our pastor who was working there.

I glance into the mirror
Behold! What do I see?
Is this really myself—
Or but an image of me?

I then half turn to go,
But turning yet remain,
Another look starts me
Contemplating on my pain.

While deeply engrossed in this picture,
A thought springs to my mind.
Be true to thine ownself—
But my true self I can't seem to find.

I am blinded by whos and whys,
As I struggle so hard to see.
Not content with another's opinion,
Wanting desperately, God, to be me.

One day my eyes shall be opened.
I shall gaze through the mist and the haze,
To see my true self in the mirror,
A reflection worthy of praise.

More Than Just the Blues

Depression is a difficult term to define. It is used to cover a wide spectrum of emotional life—from normal mood swings to severe depressive illness. Although some depression is normal, for an estimated ten to twenty million Americans it is more than just a case of the blues or a few bad days. It is a debilitating illness and a potential killer.

Some of us who suffer can identify the depression because we feel sad, unhappy—really in the pit. Others are bothered with symptoms such as insomnia, fatigue, loss of appetite, headache, stomachache, various other vague aches and pains, or irritability, without the deep melancholy. Persons with these symptoms are often surprised when a doctor tells them they are depressed.

It's amazing how many suggestions may be given to the severely depressed person. I remember being told to pull myself together or just buck up—or worse, just have faith! Of course not only did none of that help, but it probably hindered my recovery because I was already guilt-ridden for not being able to do it that way. I remember being told to go out and buy myself a new hat. Well, that's great if it works, but in severe depression I didn't care whether or not I had a hat; I didn't even care whether or not I had a head! And once I was told to go out and get drunk. How's that for problem solving? Suggestions such as these are not only harmful to the depressed person, but they also point to the widespread lack of understanding of the nature of depressive illness.

My father-in-law, who had a hearing problem, once said to me, "If a person is blind, others are sympathetic. But if a person is deaf, others are irritated." I find that reaction similar to the way people react to those who have emotional illness. If a person has high blood pressure, stomach ulcers, or one of the other illnesses that are sometimes emotionally induced, people are sympathetic. But when a person is depressed, the tendency is to blame and criticize, often with the attitude, "I don't know what you're depressed about. You should be grateful for your blessings."

There are always those who expect a depressed person to just "snap out of it." But it doesn't usually work that way. Although we are advised that all depression has a tendency toward spontaneous remission, depression usually ends only after a number of months or even years of wear and tear on the individual or after treatment or . . . suicide.

Some people are still uninformed of the fact that depression can be biochemical. Many who suffer mentally have a neurochemical disease, and it cannot be turned off at will. It is not simply a mood. Science is proving that depression is significantly influenced by specific chemicals in the brain.

Dr. Mallory in his book *Untwisted Living* gives an explanation of the chemical aspect of depression that is understandable to me as a layperson. "The brain has about 14 billion cells and an infinite number of combinations of nerve endings. Chemicals called neurotransmitters are necessary to complete the right electrical connections between the cells. Research indicates that one or more of these is in short supply when we are depressed for two weeks or longer. In this respect, depression is as much a physical disease as diabetes, or tuberculosis. If the victim fails to receive proper medication, he or she has a reduced chance of getting well."

Stress may cause this malfunction in the brain cells—just as it may cause vascular problems or stomach acids that produce ulcers. But the fact remains, a clinical alteration is taking place.

Evidences of physically induced depression may be found in the depressed menopausal woman, the post-partum woman, or those who suffer from premenstrual syndrome. Also, people have become depressed following viral illnesses such as viral pneumonia, hepatitis, and infectious mononucleosis. In addition, some medications are notorious for triggering some kind of chemical imbalance thereby producing depression.

Doctors and scientists are also finding that just as some physical handicaps are passed from generation to generation, some mental illnesses may in part be the result of the arrangement of genes and chromosomes. Dr. Mallory stated in a lecture that three or four people out of a thousand will have bipolar illness, but if they have a sibling with it their chances go to 20 to 25 percent; and if they have an identical twin with it, the chances soar to 65 to 90 percent.

Also, relatives of depressed people are more inclined to be depressed. For example, I can count seven persons on my father's side of my family, spanning three generations, who have been treated by psychiatrists.

Our genetic makeup may predispose us to depression or other negative feelings in the same way it may predispose us to physical handicaps or illnesses.

It's Rough

Depression has been classified in many ways. Dr. John White's *The Masks of Melancholy* shows depressive illness categories as shown in figure 1.

Primary depressions are mood disorders that are not associated with any other form of mental or physical illness, nor with conditions like alcoholism, homo-sexuality, or the like. The distinction is made because we do not know the effect of physical illness on depression. It is best to be clear whether or

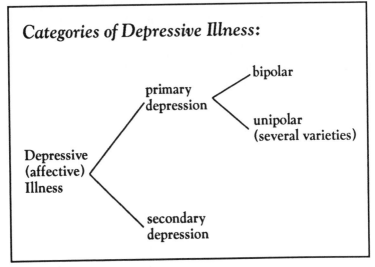

Figure 1.

not we are dealing with primary depressions (depression in "pure culture," so to speak).

Secondary depressions, on the other hand, are those that arise in the course of the illness or conditions mentioned.

Bipolar depressions are primary depressions that are characterized not only by plunges into despair but also by ascents into euphoria and even manic excitement. It is the illness that once was called manic-depressive psychosis.

Unipolar depressions (it is suspected that there are several varieties of these) do not combine highs as well as lows, but, as their name suggests, are plunges into darkness relieved only by elevation into normal moods.

To merit the description of depressive illness all of these conditions must last at least a month, and usually last much longer.

Depressive illness is extremely complex, but for the one who has it, it's rough! The pain of depression has been compared to that of a broken leg, but as one who has known depression in varying degrees I would be inclined to think that the pain goes beyond that because of the intense hopelessness involved. Depressed people usually don't think they'll ever be well. That's part of the nature of depression. And the helplessness in the minds of those who have the illness, and those who love and wait beside them, is incalculable.

Help for the Depressed

Robert Louis Stevenson is said to have been sitting out on his porch one evening when he was a little boy. As he sat there watching the night move slowly in, he saw the lamplighter coming down the street. Fascinated at seeing the old man light each light, Robert jumped up and burst into the house calling to his mother, "Hey, Mother, come quick. There's a man out here poking holes in the darkness."

Since my depression has improved significantly, I want to poke holes in the darkness for as many other people as I possibly can. I talk with numbers of depressed people in my travels and the question I hear most is, "What can I do to help?" I wish there was an easy answer, but the solution to depression is complex and varied, differing with each individual. There are, however, some frames of mind and guidelines that we can follow to greatly increase our chances of getting over depression and remaining non-depressed. I would like to share here some that I have used and found helpful.

I realize this is elemental, but let me lay a little groundwork for my "helps" by mentioning that there are three primary contributors to our makeup: the genetic, the environmental (early childhood), and the circumstantial (what is going on around us every day). There is nothing we can do about our genetics or what happened to us in childhood except to be aware of how they have possibly affected us. But there is a great deal we can do with the circumstances; and this is the area in which we work to maintain a depressed-free life.

When I talk to depressed people, I suggest that they get help from a minister, a physician, or a psychological counselor. If they are significantly depressed, it is best if they do not try to go it alone. Which "helper" one goes to depends on the individual need and the competence of available counsel.

I also encourage people in the fact that antidepressants can be helpful when the doctors say they are needed. If the depression is a medical illness, it needs a medical solution. Antidepressants work on the principle of reduced neurotransmitters (amines) in the brain. They are merely corrective; therefore they do not produce a false high and are not addictive. Many kinds of antidepressants have been on the market for years now and have been proven to be effective in a large number of cases.

In 1986, because of some serious personal stresses, I got into a depression I couldn't get out of. After it became obvious that I wasn't going to work through it by myself, I took a prescribed antidepressant. I started on a low dosage, graduated to the needed therapeutic level, remained there for several weeks, then backed out gradually. It took care of that episode of depression with minimal side effects.

In addition to suggesting outside help and medication when it is indicated, I encourage depressed people to take a good, honest look at their life, paying close attention to their responses in important relationships. The everyday things that matter are the ones that get us.

I further offer to those who suffer depression the suggestion that spending quality time with family is therapeutic. Faithfully working with them on the conflicts that arise is strengthening for the family, and for the depressed individuals as well.

People who are prone to depression usually do not assert themselves well. But we've learned that it is advantageous for us to confront others when we have been mistreated in some way. When we do it lovingly and tactfully it is usually beneficial in more than one way. It gets the conflict out in the open where it can be faced and dealt with. It also helps us to feel better about ourselves, and usually invokes respect and better treatment for us.

I have already dealt with anger, but I mention it again because it is such a biggie when it comes to depression. Many therapists believe that anger expressed and/or unexpressed is the basis for all depression. When I am depressed I search for the feelings I'm having that I don't want to have. Often these feelings are manifestations of anger and resolving them helps ease the depression.

Another wholesome practice is that of tempering our expectations of others, bearing in mind that our expectations might be excessive. Jesus gave us the "others first" concept, and this practice benefits the one who is willing to defer as much as the one to whom he defers.

I believe we are strengthened when we make a firm commitment to reality in our lives. When we see life as it really is—difficult and painful—we are on our way to health. As a maid said to her employer one day, "Life is just so daily." We're inclined to think that when we get through this problem, things will be fine. Then we find that when we finally do get through this problem, another one is just around the corner waiting its turn to do us in. We run from pain because we simply do not want to hurt—nobody does. Yet nearly all of us will admit that we've learned our most valuable lessons in the dark times. Frank said, "Those things that hurt, instruct." So the time to be happy is now. There is no dress rehearsal—this is it! The longer we wait for someone to sprinkle us with the "fairy dust of happiness," the longer we delay the maturing process and thus the wholeness we so desperately want.

Along the line of reality, I'd like to share something I learned about telling myself the truth. It is my bent, because of my low self-esteem, to tell myself things that are not only faithless, but untrue. This practice is second nature to me, yet it is so detrimental. Negative self-talk occurs in many ways; let me illustrate how it works.

If I find myself among a group of people whom I respect, I will usually worry and say to myself, "O dear, I'm the dumbest one in the crowd." This is probably not true, and even if it were it's okay because I'm okay the way I am.

Another type of negative self-talk goes something like this. I plan to take a trip so I say, "With my luck, the plane will crash." My mentality is, "I'm just old novocain lips; everything I kiss drops dead." I put myself down with this kind of talk, building in lies that insinuate that God built some kind of junk when He created me. I infer that I am unworthy of having anything good happen to me.

I have lied to myself in some other ways—some I've hated to admit, for I've said things like:

"Nobody should reject me—everybody ought to like me."

"I shouldn't have to be unhappy, and others should try to make my life happy."

"I must please everybody."

"I must always be right."

"It's terrible to feel self-conscious or nervous."

What a trip these lies put on me. Situations can be unpleasant, but they're not terrible or devastating. Only what we feel about them is devastating.

As people—severely depressed, mildly depressed, or non-depressed—we sometimes lie to ourselves in extremely serious ways, such as telling ourselves things like:

"If I fail, I will never forgive myself."

"If there is a divorce, I will never get over it."

"If this person dies, I cannot make it."

We set ourselves up with godless self-talk that creates painful and destructive emotions. Psychiatrist Wilard Gaylin said, "A denigrated self-image is a tar baby. The more we play with it, embrace it, the more bound we are to it." The best cure for this is honesty before God. Getting at raw truth about what matters to Him will free us up to be happy and productive. Jesus said, "I am the way and the truth and the life." Out of my personal experience, I strongly encourage folks to strive for truth—God's truth—in their thinking.

As we seek to understand our feelings we need to give attention to our behavior as well. We have little control over our feelings—sometimes we just have to feel them. But our behavior is under the control of our wills. We choose our behavior. It is important that we take responsibility for our reactions to life's conflicts, realizing that we are not robots; we are involved in what's happening to us emotionally and situationally. Being "done unto" is certainly not the whole picture, and we cannot pawn off on somebody else the responsibility for our happiness and good mental health.

Another thing I encourage people to do is to open up to new ideas, or maybe even change their life-style. In our fears, we are inclined to live with a tightfisted mentality that limits our involvement and our learning and, consequently, our growth. On the other hand, when our minds are open we are in a better position to learn new things that God wants to teach us. We can find new ways to cope and we can begin new habits that will help us. This might mean making changes in the time we go to bed, the time we get up, where or how we spend our waking hours. It may mean a shift in emphasis, giving more time to things we've formerly slighted or neglected. We might have to extend ourselves more, making the necessary social contacts to keep us moving out from ourselves. We may need to employ some self-improvement techniques by reading and studying the experiences of others, and listening with sensitive ears to what is going on around us. Openness could mean our rejection of some old ideas, or the acceptance of new ones. God will lead each individual in His own way.

Because our physical and mental well-being are so closely related, we do well to give attention to our bodies. A good, well-balanced diet is important. Too many simple carbohydrates can get us feeling bad—even depressed. (When I get careless about limiting my sugar intake, I feel it in an adverse way every time.) On the other hand good dietary habits boost good feelings.

A program of regular exercise is strongly recommended for everyone who is able, and it is particularly beneficial for folks with a bent toward depression. Experience shows that people who engage in some kind of aerobic exercise (such as swimming, jogging, brisk walking, or jumping rope) for at least forty minutes, four times a week, seem to have a greater protection from depression than those who take random or general exercise. There seems to be something about the rhythmic movement of the aerobics that alters body chemistry in a favorable way.

We can employ options that will provide good surroundings and relieve external stresses. If we are involved in too many activities, we can curtail them. If we have too much responsibility, we can find a way to reduce it. If we are over-worked, we can look for a way to cut down on the number of hours we work. The point is, we can alter our environment for good and decrease our stresses by managing our circumstances in a positive way.

I wish I could tell you that Christians are immune to depression, but that would be grossly dishonest. Still, receiving Jesus Christ as personal Savior and following His teachings is our greatest privilege and necessity no matter what our emotional condition. Although the acquiring of relief from psychological pain is not a worthy motive for receiving Christ, it can be a marvelous by-product because union with Christ provides the best possible basis for maturity that will result in emotional wholeness. Then, too, Christians have the spiritual and scriptural resources to lift them up. We receive salvation in Christ as the result of our volitional trust in Him and He then becomes our ultimate security because His strength and power are at work in us. The life hid in Christ is the best possible life regardless of circumstances.

When I was struggling with my deepest depression I looked for Scriptures that assured me of my salvation. A verse that helped is "If you confess with your mouth 'Jesus is Lord,' and believe in your heart that God raised him from the dead, you will be saved" (Rom. 10:9). I was so relieved when I saw that feelings are not mentioned in Scripture with regard to salvation.

There is great security in relying on the promises of God and knowing that we are cleansed of sin, kept in His love, and assured of peace if we claim it. A good verse for our meditation is John 16:33: "In me you may have peace. In the world you will have trouble. But take heart! I have overcome the world." Having peace and being an overcomer are goals for us all—it is promised in Jesus Christ.

82

Sometimes reading the Bible is difficult when we are depressed—in fact when we read it, we tend to find new ways to accuse ourselves and increase our false guilt. Yet this is God's Word to us and when it is interpreted correctly it is liberating and soothing. So I recommend meditation on the positive Scriptures when depressed. If we find it hard to concentrate, we can review the easy-to-understand, short promises of God until we are feeling better. In time, as the depression lifts, we can study more widely. I'm sure it's okay with God when we must opt for this kind of Bible study, for His yoke was meant to be easy, and His burden light.

Attending church can also be difficult for us when our anxiety levels are elevated. Yet He has told us not to forsake His house, and I'm sure He honors our obedience to this. It is good to make every effort to attend worship services. I never quit going to church through all my years of struggle. Sometimes I sat in the back and nursed my neurosis by keeping my eyes on the nearest exit. And I've worried over the typical thoughts, "What if I cry out or break and run." But I never did, and I never saw anybody else do it either. We just get frightened of our thoughts, especially those that concern possible inappropriate behavior.

There is another advantage in going to church when you're hurting. Fellow believers support and undergird in times of stress. Sure, some of them say the wrong things sometimes, but they usually want to help, and learning to live among all people is part of our maturation process. We all need friends who will accept us and share our hurts. Solomon said, "Two are better than one, because they have a good return for their work: If one falls down, his friend can help him up. But pity the man who falls and has no one to help him up" (Eccl. 4:9–10). Having friends and being a friend is good therapy. We need each other, and within the Body of Christ we can find good friends.

What about prayer? Well, if you don't feel like praying, talk to God about it. A kind of futility hovers over our prayers at times. I think we all experience some of that, whether we've had deep depression or not. Believe me when I say that I know how terribly disconcerting it is. God understands it, though, and it isn't necessary for us to pray in any special way when we're hurting . . . except maybe to be sure we pray *honestly*, and try to lay hold of the truth that God loves us and cares about our pain.

I think that learning to benefit from comforting prayer is congruent with learning the nature of God. I believe one reason praying is difficult is because we haven't really grasped the full meaning of His love, His kindness, His forgiveness. He is constantly guiding and watching over us. He is for us! He is for all of us! We tend to quit trusting God when He doesn't meet our agenda. Our faith does not make room for trusting when bad things happen to us. We need to stretch our faith, verbalize our praise and thanksgiving, our confession, and our petitions to God, whether we feel like it or not. In time, because of His faithfulness, He will help us with the feelings. On the basis of His Word, I can promise you that He always hears and answers when we pray.

"For the Lord has heard my weeping. The Lord has heard my cry for mercy; the Lord accepts my prayer" (Psalm 6:8–9).

God has given us the opportunity and the freedom to choose much in life. This is true in spiritual, psychological, and physical matters. He is closer to us than our breath, ready to guide and bless us as we are making the choices. Our pain, our confusion, our utter bewilderment can be lessened—and possibly removed—when we make correct choices of attitudes and actions.

In concluding our list of "helps" I would like to emphasize that through it all we need to be patient. Oh how hard it is to be patient! All who are involved in the difficulty—the sufferer, family, friends, counselor—all must be patient. The road to recovery can be a long one. Depression doesn't come about in a few days, and it usually will not leave in a few days.

As we try to follow good commonsense guidelines, looking to God, we can poke holes in the darkness and learn to walk in His sustaining light. There is much that can be done, everything to be gained, and every reason to be encouraged. We may get depressed, but, thank God, depression doesn't have to be the end.

Let's Hear It For the Neurotic

People with deep emotional struggles who have learned to live creatively in order to deal with their problems show a great deal of courage. I have heard more than one psychiatrist express admiration for patients who just keep gutting it out even though they often feel horrible. There are times when just to get up and get going in the morning takes more faith than a well person is called on to exercise in a month. And many neurotic people have made significant contributions to our society through the years.

Dr. John White warns that "we be cautious of judgmental attitudes toward men and women struggling beneath the weight of depression, and of glib and inaccurate explanations of their condition . . . the godliest of men and women have been gripped by profound depression."

Often obsessive, compulsive people are highly motivated and get a great deal accomplished. People we see as high achievers are sometimes neurotic personalities driven on because of feelings of personal failure.

From every walk of life we see people who have emotional difficulties. The great statesman Abraham Lincoln was reported to suffer the "black moods." Winston Churchill said of his own depression, "It follows me like a black dog." Edgar Allan Poe's poetry reflects depression, and Edward Gibbons, author of *The Decline and Fall of the Roman Empire*, is said to have had a severe depression following the completion of his book.

Martin Luther, John Bunyan, and Charles Spurgeon were bothered by depression. William Cowper, composer of "There Is a Fountain Filled With Blood," suffered depression.

We can identify great mood swings in the psalmist David as he wrote: "How long, O LORD? Will you forget me forever? How long will you hide your face from me? How long must I wrestle with my thoughts and every day have sorrow in my heart?" (Ps. 13:1–2). "Why, O LORD, do you stand far off? Why do you hide yourself in times of trouble?" (Ps. 10:1).

Then David comes back to confidently say, "The LORD is my shepherd, I shall not be in want" (Ps. 23:1). And "The LORD is my light and my salvation—whom shall I fear?" (Ps. 27:1). And then: "Sing joyfully to the LORD" (Ps. 33:1).

Hear Habakkuk cry, "O LORD, how long must I call for help before you will listen? I shout to you in vain; there is no answer. 'Help, Murder!' I cry, but no one comes to save" (Hab. 1:2 LB).

After God responds to Habakkuk, sharing something of His purpose and intent, Habakkuk sings a prayer of praise before the Lord and closes the book: "Even though the fig trees are all destroyed, and there is neither blossom left nor fruit, and though the olive crops all fail, and the fields lie barren; even if the flocks die in the fields and the cattle barns are empty, yet I will rejoice in the LORD; I will be happy in the God of my salvation. The LORD God is my Strength, and he will give me the speed of a deer and bring me safely over the mountains" (Hab. 3:17–19 LB).

And do you recognize these words? "My soul is overwhelmed with sorrow to the point of death" (Mark 14:34).

Because Jesus knew deep suffering and sorrow, He understands us.

6

IDENTIFICATION

A Necessity

On more than one occasion I had heard my friend Janice confidently state, "I know who I am." I knew she did, but I was not sure I knew exactly what she meant. And worse, I was not sure I knew who I was in the sense in which she spoke.

The following incident helped answer that for me: I was attending the closing luncheon of a writers' conference. As I took my seat at the table, somewhat late, I noticed a nice-looking man sitting on my left. We introduced ourselves in the friendly style of the conference, and he asked me a number of questions concerning my writing and what I was presently working on.

When I told him I was working on a book, he asked the obvious, "What is your book about?" Although I felt a little tender about the subject, I told him it would be on anxiety and depression. With this, his interest accelerated.

More questions came, and he was asking my opinion about a number of things related to my subject. I became delighted with his interest and was answering right along, feeling more and more at liberty to give my amateur's opinion. I gradually moved from general, appropriate responses to what you might call "shooting off my mouth."

As soon as I climbed out on the proverbial limb, it occurred to me that he was quizzing me, and I started to counter. I asked him if he had some involvement with my subject.

With just the right amount of control and a "Here's your chance" glance from his wife across the table, my new friend announced, "I am a medical doctor."

Completely disarmed and embarrassed I felt the blood start for my head. Overreacting, I made several run-together remarks intended to make myself look better. Fortunately someone called me to the telephone at just the right moment, and I excused myself from the table.

Whisking across the conference grounds to the building where the telephone was, I began to review and put into perspective the fiasco at the table. I felt that this gentleman had deliberately encouraged me to speak on matters concerning which he was much more qualified than I, and then had delighted in humiliating me. I also knew that it was my own fault; I had asked for it.

When I returned to my place at the table, I politely spoke again to the doctor, "I am sorry I reacted so defensively a few minutes ago, but I felt that you had tricked me."

It was a good lesson for me, and I am sure I won't be so quick to rattle off my opinions next time. But it served me in an even more important way. In my introspection I was able to be honest in identifying my emotions. I had first felt proud. Then I had felt deceived, ridiculed, embarrassed, and angry. This was followed by regret for my reactions, a desire to apologize, and a freedom to confront the other person (definitely new territory for me). Importantly I was able to see my actions over against God's desire for my behavior as exemplified by Jesus Christ.

I felt no need to deny my emotions (all emotions are valid) or keep up a pretense, but I could express myself openly and honestly without fear of rejection.

A sense of satisfaction over "having arrived" oozed within my spirit. I was in touch with myself. I knew who I was. And I knew that I knew.

Bruce Larson in *The One and Only You* says, "When I can say to people, 'This is what I am,' and not have to defend myself, I can begin to appreciate (others) and, incidentally, become a more well balanced person."

Learning something about who I am was important to my mental health. It was like finding my balance, gaining ability to evaluate a situation and make mature decisions, being able to trust my own judgment. It contributed to my stability and self-assurance.

As we learn our identity, we can begin to gain strength in our weak areas and move on to accept ourselves. The result is that we are happier, more comfortable to be with. We also have greater credibility and are in a better position to help other people.

It must be said, however, that finding one's self is not a cut-and-dried, once-and-for-all accomplishment, for we are people in process—becomers. Those of us who are Christians know that we are growing up in Jesus. And, from time to time, we have to reevaluate as we move along in our lives. We need to get our bearings again, for circumstances change, goals and needs change—we change.

The True Revelation

It seems to me that it would be impossible for one to find true identity without finding it in God, our Maker. It was God who created us; He knows us. It was He who dropped the plumb by which thoughts and deeds are to be measured. It is by looking at Him that we keep our equilibrium. Any scheme or design of human beings would result in chaos because of our inherent selfishness. But when we clearly see Jesus Christ, we see pure love; we see joy, peace, and caring. In Him we can know right and wrong. We can observe true perfection because He lived an exemplary life for us to follow. He is our pivot. I don't believe we know who we are until we know Him and place ourselves alongside Him.

In *The Healing of Persons*, Paul Tournier says, "The Bible records the life and death of Jesus Christ, the God-man, who knew all our physical, psychic, and spiritual difficulties, and who alone, through his perfect obedience, resolved them all. He is the true Revelation; living in personal fellowship with him we see what our personal problems are, and above all we find the supernatural strength we need to supplement our own poor efforts to resolve them. Finally, through his sacrifice on the Cross, he brings us supreme deliverance, taking upon himself all the wrongs that our efforts have failed to put right, and granting us God's forgiveness."

If we are Christians, we have a head start in the matter of self-identification. We know from the Bible that we have been made in the image of God Himself. Out of His love for us, God has made us special. Isaiah realized this too: "Let me tell you how happy God has made me! For he has clothed me with garments of salvation and draped about me the robe of righteousness. I am like a bridegroom in his wedding suit or a bride with her jewels" (Isa. 61:10 LB). The Bible also tells us that we are children of the King, joint heirs with Christ, and part of the royal priesthood.

Years ago when I worried so much about who I was, a friend quoted something her mother said to her when she was growing up. I can hear her now—her voice pitched an octave higher than usual because of the emotion she felt when she quoted it. "Now don't you forget who you are. You are a royal child of the King."

Remember the words to the old hymn:

I once was an outcast, stranger on earth,
A sinner by choice, and an alien by birth,
But I've been adopted, my name's written down,

An heir to a mansion, a robe, and a crown.
I'm a child of the King,
A child of the King;
With Jesus my Savior,
I'm a child of the King.

—Harriet E. Buell

What an inheritance! What an identification!

7

ASKING WHY

A Learning Experience

During the years of my struggle toward good mental health, one question that demanded an answer was, why do people become ill with anxiety and depression? I have come to realize there is no single universal answer. Because of human variables, there are about as many reasons for depressive illness as there are people with the problem, for each person is a composite of his or her chemistry, temperament, personality, environmental influences, and spiritual framework. We reap the result of the combination. Even though there are some general conclusions, rules of thumb, causes and effects, and some classic cases, in the final analysis each person has his or her own reason for becoming psychologically ill.

It's Okay to Ask Why

Obviously I am not a professional counselor. On the contrary I'm more of a professional patient! Yet I believe that I can safely say that when we are involved in deep struggle we are responsible to ask "why" of our own condition. It is in seeking reasons why that we find solutions and move on in health and maturity. When we are afraid to walk back into the past and lack what it takes to cope with the present or dread the future, it is time to ask why.

I have met depressed Christians who feel it is wrong to question why. They seem to have adopted the old saying "ours is not to reason why, ours is but to do or die." And they butt heads with their depression month after month, year after year, until their unhealthy patterns become so crystallized that any improvement is difficult. And they do it with sincerity in their hearts and with wills that are given to God. I have seen Christians who have resisted even the treatment of Christian psychiatrists, believing that to be in psychiatric counseling would be contrary to the will of God and spiritual Christian living. Nothing could be less true. As much as God would not want us to remain ill with pneumonia when a cure is available, so too He does not want us to suffer depressive illness when good health is available through counseling.

We must remember that most probably our roots of depression have been with us longer than our knowledge of God. And we need guidance in dealing with our depression when it robs us of our mental and spiritual peace.

As Christians our first inclination when we become emotionally disturbed is to go to our pastor, and this is good. In many instances pastoral counseling is all that is needed. In other cases, due to the nature of the problem, the help of a mental health professional is needed as well. Ideally, pastoral counseling and psychiatry or psychology go hand in hand, each recommending the other as the need is recognized. It is important that Christians be aware that depression is not always *just* a spiritual problem. Some people *do* become spiritually depressed, and are completely restored when the spiritual conflict is resolved. Countless others, however, have psychological or medical problems and, consequently, a need for psychological and/or medical treatment.

Dr. John White speaks to this: "Unfortunately, Christians tend to see their depression only in spiritual terms. They feel they have let God down. Religious Jews do the same, interpreting their experiences from within a religious framework. And spiritual counselors, caught up in the same thought frame, may rightly diagnose a spiritual problem in one client but miss a depressive illness in another so that faith is encouraged when faith is impossible, or praise encouraged from a heart as withered as a prune."

God wants us to be whole persons with healthy bodies, minds, and spirits. Good psychotherapy helps us to understand ourselves so that when we are restored those of us who choose to proceed with God may do so in a healthier, more productive way.

I Could Have Missed the Healing

Years ago when I first began to realize that I had a psychological problem, I was reluctant to look for a psychiatrist because I was afraid he would either try to make me give up my Christianity or try to convince me that my commitment to Christ was a mistake. Back then, as far as I knew, there were no Christian psychiatrists available. That meant we had to look for a qualified, reputable, professional person and trust God for the rest.

The doctor whom my family chose was well known and respected in his field, but as far as I know, he did not profess to be a Christian. He and I never had an in-depth discussion about Christianity, the Bible, or moral values. He knew that I was troubled over my relationship to God, but he considered it a symptom. His explanation to Grover was that when I was better, I would be able to get a better perspective spiritually. He mentioned that he would not attempt to discuss the Bible with me because he felt that I knew the Bible better than he did.

He then simply treated my depression with electroshocks and sent me home. Although this may not have been the first choice of treatment of many, and I needed further counseling, the point is that if I had resisted his assistance because he did not give me a Christian testimony, I could have limited God's methods and missed His healing, for my illness had reached a near psychotic stage.

I urge depressed people who have elected to see a psychiatrist to look for one who is a Christian. When a Christian psychiatrist is not available, however, and the victim of depression is not getting any better with the help of Christian friends or pastor, I do not try to dissuade them from seeing a good, reputable non-Christian rather than continuing in debilitating suffering. When a person is dangerously depressed, medication and advice that does not encourage immoral values is a better option than the result of a spiraling depression. God is in control of a Christian's life, and He can guide even in a less than preferable situation.

Let me quote from an article by O. Quentin Hyder, M.D., a Christian psychiatrist writing for the *Christian Herald*. "Whether or not the doctor writing the prescription is a Christian is beside the point—the same as with pneumonia or a broken leg. The patient must first be restored to health by the best medical means available. The psychotically depressed person must get back in touch with reality. Once that has been accomplished by drugs, hospitalization, or even shock therapy, *then* follow-up counseling can begin, preferably by a fellow Christian who has had professional counseling."

Interestingly, I have on occasion asked people if their psychiatrist was a Christian and they have replied, "I think he must be."

God does work in unexpected ways. In fact, I have prayed for His leadership in countless matters and found that He rarely answers in the way I had anticipated. Rather He chooses unique ways to help me, and I have considered all of my healing as being from God.

That I May Know Him

As I have been unraveling my story on these pages, I have shared my understanding of the psychological reasons for my depression. Simply put—the reason for my depression is that I am me. I became ill because I have the makeup that is mine, because my circumstances have fallen as they have, and because I reacted as I did.

In my quest for help, however, I was also asking a spiritual question. Why did God allow my depression? For what possible good could He use my suffering?

I believe that God had much to teach me through my depressive illness. Much of what I learned could only have been learned in my difficult circumstances. J. R. Miller in his book *Words of Comfort* says, "We do not know how much we owe to suffering. Many of the richest blessings that have come down to us from the past are the fruit of sorrow and pain."

God used my depression to teach me more about Jesus. It is one thing to be acquainted with a person, but it is quite another to really know that person. Jesus Christ is a person I needed to know intimately.

Once, while thinking about the commandment Jesus said was the first and most important: "Love the Lord your God with all your heart and with all your soul and with all your mind and with all your strength" (Mark 12:30), I realized that was a lot of loving and in all honesty I was not measuring up in my love for God. As this realization became a concern, I sought the counsel of an older Christian friend and confessed this to her, adding that I really didn't know what to do about it.

"Martha, dear," (she'd called my name that way so many times) "it is only as we know the Lord that we can love Him as we should. Just begin to pray this prayer, 'Lord, I know that I don't love You the way I should. But I want to learn to love You more. Help me to get to know You better.' " Then she told me to thank Him and go about the business of getting to know

Him through Bible study, prayer, and living in His presence each day, being sensitive to His Spirit.

This advice became the center of my quest, the center of my praying. God has said in the Bible that if we seek Him, we will surely find Him. And He is faithful to His word. He has used my depression to teach me new and wonderful things about Himself, and it has so enriched my life that I have reached the place where I can sincerely thank Him for my difficult experiences.

In getting to know Him, perhaps the most valuable thing I learned was that the scope of His love is so much wider than I had ever imagined. His limitless love, mercy, kindness, and acceptance are greater than my mind can conceive. His infinite wideness cannot be narrowed by my concept.

The words of Frederick W. Faber's great hymn say it so well:

> *There's a wideness in God's mercy,*
> *Like the wideness of the sea;*
> *There's a kindness in His justice*
> *Which is more than liberty,*
>
> . . . .
>
> *For the love of God is broader*
> *Than the measure of man's mind;*
> *And the heart of the Eternal*
> *Is most wonderfully kind.*

I believe God wanted me to learn something of His wideness so I would know that He accepts me—not because I earn it, but because He is who He is.

Our daughter Becky has taught me a lesson in acceptance. I guess it is always hard for a mother to visualize her "babies" in responsible positions. So, as Becky entered her internship with the mentally handicapped, I approached her, as a dutiful mother would, to be sure that she had carefully considered what she was doing. "Becky," (I sounded just like a mother) "do you really accept those people?"

"Accept 'em?" she asked with a little agitation in her tone, "I don't accept 'em, I like 'em."

Becky's acceptance of these exceptional people had become a foregone conclusion for her; she never even thought about it. She just knew she liked them, and she could fill some of their needs.

This is just the way it is with God. His acceptance of me is total and complete. He is not sitting in a heavenly place somewhere choking down the person of Martha Maughon; He embraces me—He likes me—with all of my failings. It is exactly this kind of loving acceptance I am commissioned to imitate as I relate to other people.

I Know How You Feel

Not only did God use my emotional illness to teach me about Himself, but He also used my suffering to make me empathetic and helpful toward other people who suffer.

The apostle Paul puts it this way: "Praise be to the God and Father of our Lord Jesus Christ, the Father of compassion and the God of all comfort, who comforts us in all our troubles, so that we can comfort those in any trouble with the comfort we ourselves have received from God" (2 Cor. 1:3–4).

Because I have traveled the steep, grim road of depression, I can say to others, "I know how you feel" and be believed. I have had opportunity to counsel with a number of people and encourage them in their quest for a healthy, happy emotional life. God with me, I can reach back and help the next person. And that's what it's all about.

The book of Hebrews also expresses the truth that our personal struggles and pain have value for others: "So take a new grip with your tired hands, stand firm on your shaky legs, and mark out a straight, smooth path for your feet so that those who follow you, though weak and lame, will not fall and hurt themselves, but become strong" (Heb. 12:12 LB).

The Treasures of Darkness

A lady once wrote me a letter in response to an article I had written on the subject of emotional illness, and in it she shared what has become a very special verse for me.

"I will give you the treasures of darkness, riches stored in secret places, so that you may know that I am the Lord, the God of Israel" (Isa. 45:3).

There are treasures in the dark places, and I can testify that they do help us to know the Lord God of Israel. And these treasures are part of God's answer when I plead, "Why am I crying?"

8

GETTING OLDER

A Reidentification

Turning fifty was a virtual zero hour for me. It represented the onslaught of all that is old. The trauma of this milestone came from more than one source.

From birth to age 18, a girl needs good parents.
From 18 to 35, she needs good looks.
From 35 to 55, she needs a good personality.
From 55 on, she needs good cash.

This bit of prose attributed to the late Sophie Tucker is not exactly a spiritual evaluation, but it does point out that we live in levels and reach stages in our lives when we have to acknowledge where we are, shift gears, and begin again.

Nobody Loves You When You're Old and Gray

I have tender memories of my grandmother. She was often in our home when I was growing up, and I spent many hours sitting at her knee as she described the old days. My grandmother was a lovely Christian lady, but despite this, she used to sing with conviction, "Nobody Loves You When You

Are Old and Gray." And because she seemed to mean it, this philosophy branded itself on my subconscious, ready to burn through later and condemn me as a relic that was becoming more worthless with each passing year.

As I began to leave mid-life behind, I became more and more convinced that the world exists for the young and beautiful. Certainly my grandmother was not entirely to blame. Madison Avenue does its share to greatly influence how we see ourselves. Madison Avenue would have us all twenty-one, ninety pounds, with long hair, a designer-jean figure, and smelling like Oscar what's-his-name.

As a little girl, I loved to dress up and stand in front of the mirror. I still like to dress up. I like the fun of mixing and matching clothes. I have enjoyed getting "colored beautiful" and analyzed for style.

But the difficulty is that, with passing time, looking in the mirror becomes less and less rewarding. Being a "foxy lady" gets tougher with the passing years, yet seems more urgent— especially for someone who struggles with self-esteem.

The crux of the matter for me was that as someone who had always lacked self-appreciation, I spent a lot of time and energy trying to become someone whom others appreciated.

I would love to have been Miss America!

Once I had a hilarious, technicolor dream: I was the jelly bean queen. Now I have no idea what that is, but that's what I was . . . riding on a float, smiling and waving to the admiring crowd. There were millions of vividly colored jelly beans everywhere—on the float, in the air—an extraordinary extravaganza. It was ridiculous, of course, and my family still teases me about it, but for one phantasmal moment I reigned over something. What excitement and fulfillment! What ego! What self-fascination! What evidence of low self-esteem!

Life in my forties was great. I felt good and situationally things were smooth. But with the fifties I began seeing too much change, and experiencing too much loss. Physical limitations clamored to be recognized. I often felt like the woman who said, "Everything I have ever appreciated is either turning gray, drying up, or falling out."

With these feelings of discouragement I knew it was time to reexamine and reidentify who I was as a woman. I began with my perception of physical beauty. A magazine article, "Putting Looks in Perspective," by Dr. Theodore Rubin helped me with this.

"I wonder whether society hasn't stressed the value of appearance out of all proportion. The great majority of individuals not blessed with near-perfect features may wind up feeling less than worthwhile simply because they can't live up to an unattainable ideal.

"The source of these attitudes isn't hard to identify: we're taught to value external attributes from an early age. Fairy-tale and film heroines are invariably beautiful. Pretty classmates are favored by insensitive teachers, and unthinking relatives may dote on more winsome siblings. During adolescence, peer pressure to conform to the current mode becomes stronger than ever, and this input can lead to crippling self-criticism and distorted self-perception. When these impressions are carried into adulthood, they can negatively affect competence as well as social skills; a person who believes herself to be undesirable is likely to apply that lack of confidence to other areas. What a tragic, unnecessary waste of potential!"

The sentence, "a person who believes herself to be undesirable is likely to apply that lack of confidence to other areas" aptly described what I had been doing.

Dr. Rubin's words concerning beauty were helpful to me: "Let's consider genuine beauty, which has far less to do with external packaging than with inner life: qualities such as humor, compassion, thoughtfulness, tact, insight. . . . However physically 'beautiful' any of us may be, development of the whole personality strengthens trust in self. This attitude in turn creates an inner radiance—a relaxed, accepting outlook that never fails to draw others to us. In addition, as our focus broadens, we increase our awareness of the needs and feelings of others . . . and that sensitivity is the most attractive quality there is."

The Bible also addresses the question of what true beauty is. In writing to the New Testament Christians, Peter says, "Your beauty should not come from outward adornment, such as braided hair and the wearing of gold jewelry and fine clothes. Instead, it should be that of your inner self, the unfading beauty of a gentle and quiet spirit, which is of great worth in God's sight" (1 Peter 3:3–4).

There it was—the unfading beauty of a gentle and quiet spirit, the beauty of compassion, thoughtfulness, and insight. That kind of beauty doesn't fade with age—it mellows with age. Here were some rudders to steer me in the right direction.

At dinner one night I was sitting next to Kell, a handsome college boy. During our conversation, Mildred's name was mentioned. "Isn't she beautiful!" Kell exclaimed, stretching out the sentence for emphasis. I was surprised at his comment at first, for Mildred was seventy-two years old.

L. C. Lane, one of our ministers, returned from hospital visitation with his face aglow. "You should see Mrs. Adams. She's beautiful!" Mrs. Adams was eighty-eight years old, but she had delighted and charmed this young man when he went to minister to her.

The beauty to be desired is that which comes from a love for God that is tucked tightly within our innermost beings. It is a love that donates itself freely, whether or not it invokes a response.

Very closely related to my perception of physical beauty was my need to understand my sexuality, for a very real part of the difficulty in mid-life is the fear of becoming unattractive to the opposite sex. I have discussed this with a number of people and find that it is a part of the dread of aging. In all honesty, it is natural to enjoy admiration from the opposite sex, and a woman, especially, often wonders if she will lose the admiration of her husband. But sexuality, like beauty, must be defined.

A noted psychiatrist has defined sex appeal as the ability to send out a message of acceptance, a message that promises safety, not judgment or rejection. Sexuality understood in this context is a beautiful, lifelong quality for a woman as well as a man, and it has little or nothing to do with age.

God uses our characteristics of warmth and acceptance when they are committed to Him. These are vital in our relationships to others, and they are a far cry from the warped picture of sexuality being painted by our society today.

Sexuality is one feature that helps make us who we are, and in a day when individuals are encouraged to disregard their sexual identity in favor of a more unisexual society, it is imperative that we Christians be in touch with our sexuality and use it to His glory.

Coming to an understanding of inner beauty and of my own sexuality helped me during this time in my life. But there was difficulty in other areas as well. I was experiencing a great deal of change. No one seemed to be standing still. I could see serious change in my mother. My girls had grown up. They had married and left home, and now they were having children of their own. Even Grover was changing.

With all of this change I experienced a sense of loss—not only the loss of family life as I had known it but also the loss of the assurance of my purpose and value. Even though God had already given me good insight into who I was, it seemed that a reidentification of my role—where do I go from here?—was inevitable.

The losses and the need for reidentification steadily took their toll. Eventually I became worn down by negativism, discouragement, reduced energies, and a serious estrogen deprival. These struggles led me back to counseling with Dr. Mallory. With his guidance I was able to talk about aging and about some of the heartache that comes with seeing decline in ourselves and in those we love. We talked about loss and change. In his own inimitable style, he helped me to see that autumn women still have value. He pointed out that if a woman puts all her eggs in one basket—youth and appearance maybe?—there will come a time when she will be left vacant and empty.

Then with the incontrovertible direction of the Holy Spirit, Dr. Mallory guided as I endeavored to reidentify my role as a woman and as a child of God. "As Christians," he said, "we have a distinct advantage in the matter of identification. We are God's agents of healing."

Agents of healing. It seemed so simple, yet it really spoke to my heart. In my turmoil I had lost sight of my most important role—that of healing. And the grandest thing is I will never outlive the need for healing in the lives of others. Hurting people will always be with us.

As I thought about what Dr. Mallory had said, I became more encouraged. God could use the inner beauty that He gives—thoughtfulness, compassion, insight, a gentle spirit—to be healing forces in the lives of the people around me: my family, my neighbors, my friends, other depressed people. God could take all of my experiences and use them to give my life a new direction and a new sense of purpose.

Later I read in Dr. Mallory's *Untwisted Living*: "Multitudes of people are trying to get their lives unfolded while pursuing the destructive fads and philosophies of our time. There is a desperate need for agents of healing who can intelligently and compassionately help the misguided and confused turn and start living the fulfilled life which the Creator intended. To the degree you are able to minister in this fashion, you will discover your own fulfillment and meaning in life."

The Together People

Recently I was talking with a gentleman I know only slightly. "You seem to be the typical career lady who really has it all together," he said. I could have laughed out loud for the irony of his remark.

"Nothing could be further from the truth," I confessed. "Actually, I'm a past-fifty wife, mother, and grandmother with all the frustrations that come with the job."

Later as I reflected on what had been said, I was sure God was as amused as I was. Nobody has it all together. But the Christian is a paradox. When we assume the Christlike characteristics of vulnerability and honesty about our weaknesses and failures in order to help others, when we are for real, the world usually sees us as people in control. Others feel safe with us. We are the together people. In our weaknesses we become strong.

The apostle Paul confessed that he had a thorn in the flesh. One of the sweetest things God ever did for us was not revealing what that thorn was. As far as I'm concerned, it might have been an emotional problem. The point is that even though Paul begged the Lord to remove it, God left the thorn and gave grace. "My grace is sufficient for you, for my power is made perfect in weakness" (2 Cor. 12:9).

And Paul's response to the Lord was, "Therefore I will boast all the more gladly about my weaknesses, so that Christ's power may rest on me. That is why, for Christ's sake, I delight in weaknesses, in insults, in hardships, in persecutions, in difficulties. For when I am weak, then I am strong" (2 Cor. 12:9–10).

As I reidentify at this stage of my life, I know that I am Martha, friend of Jesus. Because He lives in me, I am promised something of His beauty. Because I am committed to Him, I can be an agent of healing. And because He is committed to me, I am one of His together people . . . living in His strength, knowing my weakness.

The Case for Estrogen

Although reidentification was an important hurdle for me in my emotional maturation process, it was not the whole answer to my age-fifty crisis. My postmenopausal symptoms became insufferable.

At the onset of the climacteric of my life, I had made up my mind that I would recognize all the normal, unpleasant symptoms stemming from a changing life; I would deal with them maturely, without blaming them on a dysfunction of the hormonal system. I determined to take in stride any fear of aging, worry over the natural losses, or concern about the problems of aging parents, grown children, or any of the other possible traps that might ensnare me. After all, I was a veteran at handling emotional stress!

Unfortunately, however, these dilemmas are not always settled in our determinate wills. And even though with gritted teeth I stubbornly defied all my discomforts, I could not withstand the barrage of menopausal symptoms that besieged me.

My list of complaints became embarrassing, if not downright comical. I had insomnia, very disconcerting chest pains, weak and painful joints, the inner trembles, depleted ability to cope with the smallest crisis—and those hot flashes! They came at frequent intervals both day and night, and each one was preceded by an intolerable mental crash.

The worst of it was that I was once again severely depressed. I had lost all sense of peace; I had no ability to plan ahead or to look forward to anything. I thought of nothing but illness and death—especially my own. I was absolutely morose, a walking doomsday.

This condition, however, was unlike anything I had experienced before, for, as contrary as it may seem, I was depressed but not unhappy. My depression was chemically oriented, and this time I could identify it as such. I worked hard exercising all the things I had successfully practiced in stressful times before but with little benefit. It was wearing me down.

Estrogen Replacement Therapy (ERT) was recommended to me on several occasions, but I had steadfastly resisted because of the possible uterine cancer risk involved. It seemed that doctors were somewhat divided over the wisdom of using estrogen replacement, and I felt it would be better if I could get by without it.

Eventually the day came when I reached the miserable end of my tolerance. Knowing that sometimes we have to make a choice when all options are less than perfect, I consulted a cancer specialist. He felt that given my circumstances, taking the lowest dosage of estrogen for the shortest length of time would be a good alternative for me. It was a prayerful, careful decision, but when I began the estrogen, I was confident it was the right thing to do.

The benefits have been remarkable. Not only did my hot flashes, fatigue, and depression improve immediately, but I also became free of some of the other symptoms as well. My zest for life returned, and I regained a quality of healthy living I had not known for a long time. Since the time I began ERT, further studies have shown that estrogen given in combination with progesterone (another female hormone) is safe for the uterus. In fact, according to *Woman's Health Advisor*, there is some evidence in recent studies to suggest that women who take estrogen with progesterone are even less likely to get uterine cancer than women who aren't on hormonal therapy. (Still, women who have a history of cancer are advised to be especially cautious about using ERT.) I might add that also shown in the studies is the evidence that ERT is believed to help osteoporosis by significantly reducing bone loss. In light of these facts, I have remained on ERT longer than I had originally planned, and I continue to find it helpful for mood swings.

In *What Wives Wish Their Husbands Knew About Women* James Dobson makes a helpful contribution to this subject. "It is my opinion that many members of the medical profession (particularly those outside the speciality of gynecology) are grossly uninformed on the relationship between estrogen levels and emotional stability in women. . . . Physical dependency on estrogen for some women has far reaching psychological implications, and failure to recognize this fact can be devastating to a menopausal patient. . . . I am convinced that there are women confined in hospitals for the emotionally disturbed today who are actually suffering from hormonal deprivation." It seems to me that the number of women who experience estrogen deprival severe enough to confine them to a hospital is relatively low, but it is certainly a comfort to know that knowledgeable, respected people, such as Dr. Dobson, are aware of how severe this estrogen problem can become.

Dr. William A. Nolen wrote an article entitled, "Estrogen Therapy at Menopause: Weighing the Risks," in which he gives a very comprehensive review of the pros and cons of estrogen therapy. He includes the following statements: "The key point to consider in deciding about estrogen therapy is the severity of the problem. . . . I, and many other doctors, believe that we have publicized the dangers of estrogen therapy far out of proportion to the real risks involved."

Then Dr. Nolen quotes from an article in The Journal of Family Practice that summarizes information gathered at a National Institute of Health Conference. "The decision whether to use estrogen is not an isolated event. Rather it occurs in the context of a woman's personal history and many other, as yet incompletely understood, medical, psychological, social, and cultural factors relating to menopause and aging. Thus, the woman and her physician should confer openly and arrive together at the total approach, whether it includes estrogen use or not, most likely to promote her general well-being during the postmenopausal years."

As time slides by, bringing the inevitable changes and losses, I appreciate more and more the lovely words in Ecclesiastes: "There is a time for everything . . . a time to be born and a time to die . . . a time to tear down and a time to build . . . a time to weep and a time to laugh . . . a time to search and a time to give up . . . a time to keep and a time to throw away . . . a time to love and a time to hate" (Eccl. 3:1–8).

Just as the light of today slowly dims, only to break forth in splendor tomorrow, we too move slowly from the glow and strength of youth toward a dimness, to be raised again in eternal brilliance into "an inheritance that can never perish, spoil or fade—kept in heaven for [us]" (1 Peter 1:4).

9

GOING ON

I'll Be Okay

Everyone must cope with loss, and some of our losses are traumatic and engender deep hurt. Emma, my sister-in-law, suffered a series of heavy losses within a very short period of time. They included the loss of an eighteen-year-old son in a shooting accident as well as her husband's illness and death. If I strung out all of the sad things that went on in Emma's life at that time, she would sound like a candidate for the old TV show, "Queen for a Day." It was incredible.

A friend who had observed Emma's creative coping once asked sympathetically, "Emma, how can you go on?"

"How can I go on?" Emma echoed kindly. "There is nowhere to go but on."

We all admire people like Helen Keller or Joni Tada who plug on against insurmountable odds. Yet "everyday folks" are doing that, too. Our unsung friends and loved ones are pressing on despite their troubles.

My friend Rebecca works in our church office. I have seen her undergo the serious physical difficulty of cancer; now she is plagued with the debilitating hardship of multiple sclerosis. In spite of this Rebecca reports to work right on time every day; she takes part in many activities and continues to make positive, happy contributions to our lives. She is going on.

My daughter Janie is bothered by some of the same emotional hindrances that beset her mother. She has known a lot of disappointment in her life. Following five miscarriages, she stayed in bed seven months in order to give birth (by Caesarean section) to her little daughter . . . then nearly lost the thirteen-day-old baby to infection. Janie plans to have another child so Amanda won't have to grow up alone. Janie, too, is going on.

We can all name people we know who are going on. We all come to those times in our lives when, no matter how we feel, no matter what is happening around us, we must "load 'em up, head 'em out, Rawhide!"

After having shared my emotional pain in these pages, I could give one final shout of victory and tell you that it is all in the past. It would make a nice ending, but it would not be true.

God in His kindness has given me some insight; He has been with me in the valleys, and I do not suffer as I once did. But I'm still me. I still contend with some of my same problematic tendencies. Fear is programmed into me, and I continue to deal with it.

Recently I heard a woman say that she had been really frightened only twice in her life. I nearly fainted. I was so busy marveling at her claim that I missed what she said caused those two fear experiences. I'm so phobic and over-reactive that I don't remember two whole days in my life in which something didn't scare me—an airplane ride, deep water, rejection, disapproval, failure, poor health. For me every pain is a heart attack, and every sore place is terminal. You name it; I'm scared of it!

And I'm still looking for the BIG OKAY. Several years ago when I was the teacher for our children's church, one of my little students made an interesting comment as he was watching television. Gazing at Wonder Woman he mused, "Mother, doesn't she look just like Mrs. Maughon?"

There is certainly no resemblance between Lynda Carter and me, but this little guy thought of his teacher when he saw

Wonder Woman. He will never know how close to my heart he was, for the nagging persistency of my temperament is to be superwoman—a never-failing bionic—living my life without blemish or blunder, attempting to correct all of my problems and all the problems of the world. As my daughter so accurately put it, "Meme, you try to fix everything."

That's Life

Throughout our days we all will have to cope with stress and conflict. Pain and struggle will be part of our human experience. None of us is exempt. I've had to struggle for years to gain insights into my particular problems, and I will probably struggle during the years that lie ahead.

Blanche Kaplain, a family therapist, points out: "As feeling human beings, we'll have both positive and negative emotions until the day we die. It's not necessary to get rid of all uncomfortable feelings in order to get on with our lives. Though we may not be able to make a feeling go away, we can learn from it and can continue to change our behavior."

I must have read this beautiful poem, whose author is unknown, a hundred times or more. Each time I read it, I am deeply moved as it depicts the challenge of *going on*.

> *A tired old doctor died today, and a baby boy was born—*
> *A little new soul that was pink and frail,*
>   *and a soul that was gray and worn.*
> *And—halfway here and halfway there*
> *On a white, high hill of shining air—*
> *They met and passed and paused to speak*
>   *in the flushed and hearty dawn.*
>
> *The man looked down at the soft, small thing,*
>   *with wise and weary eyes;*
> *And the little chap stared back at him,*

with startled, scared surmise,
And then he shook his downy head—
"I think I won't be born," he said;
"You are too gray and sad!" And he shrank
from the pathway down the skies.

But the tired old doctor roused once more
at the battle-cry of birth,
And there was memory in his look of grief
and toil and mirth.
"Go on!" he said. "It's good—and bad:
It's hard! Go on! It's ours, my lad."
And he stood and urged him out of sight,
down to the waiting earth.

There have been some special times when God has chosen unique ways to assure me that I am in His hands. One such experience occurred a couple of years ago.

I'll Be Okay

I sat in the Tokyo airport and prayed that the plane would hurry. My friend Barbara and I were headed for Okinawa where the Billy Graham Evangelistic Crusades would begin in just a few days. I had joined Grover to work in Japan, but the work had kept us separated much of the time. It had been a hectic time, and as we approached the final days before the Crusade, I honestly wondered if God could use our human efforts to have a great Crusade.

I was unaccustomed to overseas work; I was exhausted, homesick, and fighting a virus. More distressing than all of that, I kept feeling those earthquakes! Although the Japanese people have lived with them all of their lives and take them in stride, they terrified me (naturally). I had already been through two big ones, and the lighter tremors just wouldn't quit. I had gotten very neurotic about those earthquakes!

I prayed from the depth of my soul, "Lord, I know this is your earth, and you can shake it anytime you want to. But will you please just keep it still until I can get on that airplane?" (Forget that I am afraid to fly; just give me the opportunity!)

Finally, we boarded. I took a window seat, and we taxied out. At last I felt our plane leave the ground. We were airborne, and I was still in one piece. I thanked God as we steadily moved away from the ground, up through the murky smog that hovered over Tokyo. I shivered as I realized I would have to return. Mr. Graham's Crusades would be held in four cities, and my greatest responsibilities would be in Tokyo. How would I ever manage?

Quite suddenly the plane broke out of the ugly veil and shot into the most glorious sunset I have ever seen—brilliant majestic color illuminated every cloud that could be seen. We were swallowed up in a blaze of beauty as the sun poured itself out high above the clouds over Japan—that country whose friend is the sun.

Out of that grandeur God impressed me with what He wanted me to know. He would have the Crusades. I would see His mighty hand at work in a marvelous way. I would come back to Tokyo, and I would be okay. I'd never had such an instantaneous lift from the pit; I praised Him for the sweet relief and confirmation.

In the days that followed I saw thousands of men, women, boys, and girls come to Christ in Okinawa, Osaka, Fukouka. Then we went back to Tokyo. There were no earthquakes to shake those thousands who gathered to hear the gospel—only the gentle swaying of the Holy Spirit in our hearts.

God does not always buoy me up on a sunset when I am feeling low, but He does promise to stay with me when my world turns dark and trembles. I will be okay in the times when I am called on to be more than I am. God will see to that.

Do You Believe This?

It was to Martha that Jesus first declared, "I am the resurrection and the life. He who believes in me will live, even though he dies; and whoever lives and believes in me will never die. Do you believe this?" (John 11:25–26).

I know that none of Jesus' declarations were made first to me. I would not take my analogy that far. But with everything that is in me, I hurl myself into Martha's magnificent confession of faith as she responds: "Yes, Lord, . . . I believe that you are the Christ, the Son of God, who was to come into the world" (John 11:27).

My friend Jesus, the Son of God, makes it possible to go on. And I pray with the weeping prophet Jeremiah, "O LORD, I know it is not within the power of man to map his life and plan his course—so you correct me, Lord; but please be gentle" (Jer. 10:23–24 LB).

When my little grandchildren come to visit me, we go through our usual ritual. I go out to meet them, stoop down, open my arms, and call them by name. They laugh hilariously with the freedom that only a child has, then they run into my arms. As I hug them tightly and tell them I love them, I think about how the hurts will come to them, and in my humanness I wish I could shield them from all the times they will cry. But I know if they miss life's struggles, they will not grow into full human beings.

I am reminded of how God stooped down from heaven in Jesus Christ. How He calls us by name and enfolds us as a mother hen gathers her little ones. How He tells us He loves us and wants us to grow through our struggles. That is why He does not hold back the agonies of life. That is why He permits us to cry.

God's heart is touched with our sorrow. We can go on, knowing that He gives grace and strength in weakness, treasures in the dark places, songs in the night, and joy in the morning.

He gives us Himself.

Hallelujah!

Note to the Reader

The publisher invites you to share your response to the message of this book by writing Discovery House Publishers, Box 3566, Grand Rapids, MI 49501, USA. For information about other Discovery House books, music, or videos, contact us at the same address or call 1-800-653-8333. Find us on the Internet at http://www.dhp.org/ or send e-mail to books@dhp.org.